"Working with Kent Phillips in a clinical setting, he has a full and valuable understanding of the Addiction world. This treatise examines multiple aspects and failures in terms of addressing the Opioid and Drug Crisis in the USA. He takes us on a journey through the foundations and expansions of drug availability in our communities, governmental failures in halting, shortcomings of our prevention programs, and the weakness of treatment protocols and therapeutics. This work is a must-read for anyone with an interest or involvement in Addiction."

BONNIE DENDOOVEN, MC, LPC, CSAT, CMAT
Author of Mawasi Index Trainer at International Institute of Trauma and Addiction Professionals

"Mr. Kent Phillips masterfully provides an insightful and comprehensive overview of the current state of opioid crisis and the overall challenges in the American addiction treatment system. Drawing from his successful business executive experience and personal recovery journey, he engages the reader in trying to find better and more efficient solutions to the deadly disease of addiction. Brilliant and thrilling, a must read!"

DR. ELENA VOLFSON, MD
Mayo Clinic
Addiction Psychiatrist
Assistant Professor of Psychiatry
Mayo Clinic Medical School

American Overdose

American Overdose

America's Addiction Crises, the Whole Story

Kent I. Phillips

RESOURCE *Publications* • Eugene, Oregon

AMERICAN OVERDOSE
America's Addiction Crises, the Whole Story

Copyright © 2019 Kent I. Phillips. All rights reserved. Except for brief quotations in critical publications or reviews, no part of this book may be reproduced in any manner without prior written permission from the publisher. Write: Permissions, Wipf and Stock Publishers, 199 W. 8th Ave., Suite 3, Eugene, OR 97401.

Resource Publications
An Imprint of Wipf and Stock Publishers
199 W. 8th Ave., Suite 3
Eugene, OR 97401

www.wipfandstock.com

PAPERBACK ISBN: 978-1-5326-8489-0
HARDCOVER ISBN: 978-1-5326-8490-6
EBOOK ISBN: 978-1-5326-8491-3

Manufactured in the U.S.A. JULY 3, 2019

AMERICAN OVERDOSE is a three-part treatise written to provide the who, what, where, when, how, and why about our national drug crisis.

AMERICAN OVERDOSE: BOOK 1
Opioids are dangerous and are the source of the expansion of addiction in the USA. How the "pushers" target suburbia, the frightening growth rate, and how government has failed us.

TREATMENT TALK: BOOK 2
A must read for those considering treatment. What is available, what works, what to expect, do's and don'ts.

KILLING FAMILY: BOOK 3
When addiction comes to visit the family, everything changes. This book is written to help everyone in the family live a healthier life, what to expect, what to accept, and what to do.

Contents

About the Author | xi
Acknowledgements and Disclaimers | xiii
Trilogy Introduction | xv
To the Reader | xvii

Book 1—American Overdose | 1

American Overdose—Introduction | 3

Section 1—The Origins | 5

The Opioid Crisis—Where Did It Come From? | 7
Self-Medication—The Beginning | 11
Hard Drug Statements—Opioid, Meth, and Cocaine | 16
The Progression | 21
The Substance Nation | 24

Section 2—How Bad Is It? | 35

The Opioid Crisis—How Bad Is It? | 37
The Clinical Side | 42
Checklist | 46
Recreational Marijuana | 48
The Addict | 52
The Process of Relapse | 56

Section 3—Conclusions | 61

Arizona-Specific Statements | 63

CONTENTS

Book 2—Treatment Talk | 67

    Treatment Talk—Prologue | 69

Section 1—Treatment in General | 73
    Introduction to the Reader | 75
    The Essence of Recovery | 78
    Sending a Child to Treatment | 82
    Who Should Go? | 95
    Rehab and Fantasies | 101
    Compliance and Surrender | 104

Section 2—Addiction Aspects | 107
    Medically Assisted Treatment | 109
    Stress Affects Your Body | 112
    Boredom | 116
    Defiance | 120

Section 3—Treatment Talk | 127
    Cell Phones | 129
    Conclusion | 134
    The Ten Commandments of Helping | 136

Book 3—Killing Family | 139

    To the Reader | 141
    Introduction | 142

Section 1—The Problem | 147
    The Predator | 149
    The Discovery | 152
    The Confrontation | 153
    The Voices of Addiction | 155
    Enabling—An Act of Love | 160

Section 2—When Addiction Strikes | 165
    The Lethality of Money | 167
    The Electric Avenue | 170
    The Evolution of the American Family | 173
    The Genetics of Addiction | 178

CONTENTS

SECTION 3—CONCLUSIONS AND CONSIDERATIONS | 183
    The Twelve Steps of AA—Fighting Addiction | 185
    The Damage of Secrets | 190
    American Overdose Trilogy—Conclusion | 193

About the Author

ADDICTION SPECIALIST KENT I. Phillips shares a lifetime of addiction experience and training. Thirty years in Alcoholics Anonymous, plus training as a BS and as a Master of Science in Addiction Counseling (MSAC). He is experienced at both the personal and the clinical level.

Born in Indianapolis, Indiana in 1946, Mr. Phillips currently resides in Phoenix, Arizona, with his wife of 45 years, two sons and two grandchildren. Mr. Phillips is a national contractor in Addiction Counseling and provides treatment protocols to multiple treatment centers.

Mr. Phillips' experience included a chair, on guitar, at SUN records studios in Nashville, management with the Pillsbury Company of Minneapolis, Minn., and founding Databank USA in 1979, a national marketing research firm. Mr. Phillips sold the corporation in 2007 and began a full life devoted to helping those with addictions. He specializes in Opioid addiction in patients less than thirty years of age.

American Overdose is an addiction trilogy, and his first with Oxford/American Publishing. The three books contained in this trilogy are *American Overdose*, discussing the drug crisis in our nation that is taking so many young lives; *Treatment Talk*, offering an in-depth analysis of treatment centers, treatment protocols, and what type of treatment to seek; and *Killing Family*, a handbook for the family to aid them in knowing what to expect, what to accept, and what to do when addiction arrives in one's life.

Acknowledgements and Disclaimers

Every thanks to my wife of 45 years, Mary Joyce. I am sorry that I was up so early working on this book every morning. Also thanks to my two sons, Timothy and Charles, for continued input and help. Also for the inspiration from Tim's wife, Josephine, for giving us the two most beautiful granddaughters in the world: Kendall and Skyler. Looking into their young eyes inspired some of this book, and wondering where we will be in ten years or so, when they enter high school or middle school.

The problem is hard drug addiction, and it is getting worse daily. Availability of substances is increasing, and the presence of dangerous addictive drugs penetrates suburban neighborhoods and rural communities. Patients of mine less than twenty-one years of age tell me it is cheaper and easier to buy heroin than a six-pack of craft beers. Drinking parties for high school aged adolescents have morphed into drug experimentation sessions. Weekend using sometimes becomes daily. Daily turns into full addiction.

These three books are a general approach to understanding addiction. Some of the chapters may seem to contain repetitive statements, and I apologize for that. The reason is that each chapter is supposed to be a reference entity, so they contain some explanations that may apply to several other chapters.

The purpose of these three books is to provide some thoughts and information for the family that is suffering from addiction. I hope that these books will provide a picture for you to help you realize that you are NOT ALONE, and that what is happening to you is becoming quite common. You are in our prayers.

Kent I. Phillips
Kipphillips46@gmail.com
Master Addiction Specialist
Phoenix, Arizona

Trilogy Introduction

THIS TRILOGY, *American Overdose*, *Treatment Talk*, and *Killing Family* is not clinical nor scientific. Each book reflects experience and statistics, and are written to help those afflicted with addiction, or suffering due to a loved one's substance abuse.

The patients of young addicts are in crisis and generally have no idea of how to deal with addiction when it comes to visit. We all want to help a loved one who became addicted to alcohol, heroin, cocaine or methamphetamens. Most of the time, the way we show our love is exactly wrong, and may hurt more than help.

Most addicts draw their sustenance from the love of another person. Addicts manipulate this love to secure money, food, and/or shelter. I suppose that not every relationship is exactly the same, but in the world of addiction, behavior is predictable. As you read these pages, this may be your first experience dealing with addiction, and you are afraid. I hope that this treatise helps you in overcoming your fears and concerns. We have seen a thousand cases, and I can assure you that most addiction events have happened again and again. Addictive Behavior is predictable. We know what is going to happen if the abuse continues.

Please do not consider these three books as clinical advise, since the need for a professional Addiction counselor, coach, or therapist is imperative. Professional help is always recommended prior to any action. I pray that these three books encourage you to understand that you are not alone, or helpless. Millions have had the same experiences as you.

Kent I. Phillips, BA, MS, MSAC

To the Reader

THESE THREE BOOKS DEAL with addiction. The first book, *American Overdose*, is a treatise on the growth and impact of drugs in the United States. The government makes declarations such as proclaiming an Opioid Overdose Crisis, but little happens. I believe we have underestimated the number of young hard drug addicts in America. We are at epidemic proportions, and legal opioid (pain pills) prescriptions have increased 400 percent in the last decade. What is alarming about this increase is the fact that pain has not increased, only the need for more prescriptions. The illegal opioids that come into the country have found a new marketplace in the last five years or so. Dealers have penetrated even the smallest community or suburb. Hard drugs are no longer just in the "inner city." Currently, the DEA, ICE, the FBI, the Coast Guard, Border Security, and the local constabulary have had little to NO effect on stemming the flow of drugs into our nation. Patients claim that prescription opioids and other drugs are are often a prelude to addiction. I am not sure what the national numbers are, but here in little old Arizona, there were 312,255 opioid prescriptions written in the month of May 2018. This is one script for every 20 people. Included in *American Overdose* are chapters that present how drug use is changing our culture and our youth. You may begin to see some of the results in your neighborhood, but don't be alarmed; addiction is growing nationwide. You are not alone.

The second book, *Treatment Talk*, is a guide to the right kind of treatment modalities and protocols and a presentation of the true statistics of recovery after treatment. The addiction treatment companies are big business, and they will not be happy with this evaluation. I suppose this book is a "consumer guide" to the different kinds of treatment, what they promise, and what one can expect. Simply, treatment efforts are failing. Most centers offer "experience based" treatment, role playing, Cognitive Behavioral Therapy, groups, and private counseling. I am sure these are fine for alcoholics, but they are *not working* for the hard drug addicted patient. We need new, innovative protocols for treatment, but these will not appear until the State Boards that control education and training, protocol proficiency, and licensing, impose new standards.

Today our educational programs in schools, our treatment plans, and aftercare are not working at all. Some will argue with this, but look at the statistics. Over 90 percent of addicts relapse after treatment. Overdose deaths have increased 70 to 80 percent so far *this year*. Some have an attitude that "these people are just bums, and are weak citizens." Nothing could be further from the truth. Although there are a few exceptions, the kids that are addicted to very hard and dangerous drugs are the best and the brightest. They experiment with a hard drug at a party, then quickly continue on to daily using. Many are top students, athletes, and community contributors. Addiction never sleeps, and it does not discriminate. To a dealer, *everyone* is a target.

The third book, *Killing Family*, is a description of how addiction destroys the mental health of the family. Included is a discussion of how hard drug distribution has penetrated the rural communities and the suburbs. Drugs are no longer just in the "inner city." In the last five years the "pushers" of substances came to the realization that there is more money to be made from addicts outside of the inner city. In our communities, adolescents will hide the truth about the availability of drugs in their schools. Saying "no, we don't have any in our school," is much easier than saying "yes." What begins with an innocent "sampling" becomes a daily habit. Our suburban and rural youth are the perfect targets for addiction. They have money, mobility, and secrecy. Data suggests that hard drug use is doubling about every twenty four months.

Killing Family is a handbook for when addiction comes to your home or that of a loved one. It presents What to Expect, What to Accept, and What to Do in detail. Most parents, when they make the "discovery" that their child is using drugs, are in shock. They are embarrassed about it, fearful of it, and have no idea what to do about it. I hope this work addresses all of these questions completely. I was a little questionable about the title *Killing Family*, as I know our friend Bill O'Reilly uses this same concept in his fabulous works such as *Killing Kennedy*, *Killing Lincoln*, etc. I recommend these books highly. It just seemed to me that *Killing Family* is exactly what drugs and addiction do. I pray that reading these books will help those in crisis.

Kent I. Phillips, BA, MS, MSAC
kipphillips46@gmail.com

BOOK 1

AMERICAN OVERDOSE

American Overdose

Introduction

THIS TREATISE DEALS WITH the origins, facts, dangers, growth of, and the current trends of America's Opioid Crisis. We are, unknowingly and unwillingly, in a war with substances that destroy people, communities, families, and civilization. More importantly, we are LOSING this war. The worst part of this war is that we are losing some of the best and brightest of our youth to addiction.

One of the alarming problems is that no one is sure who or where to attack. The enemy is very illusive, secretive, organized, and often invisible. Dangerous substances began to infiltrate into the American Landscape in the late sixties. It began with "diet pills" and "pot." Today the popular substances are cocaine, meth, and opioids(heroin). Todays substances, which I call "hard drugs" in this book, are available everywhere, require ever increasing doses over time, and eventually can kill the user. Our culture has always had alcohol consumption, and certainly alcohol by itself has caused enough problems, incarcerations, and deaths. Today's problems, with the harder drugs, are just way out of control.

The Center for Disease Control estimates that over 150 people die each day from overdoses. I think this number is low, since it relies upon accurate reporting from emergency rooms. Even so, as a point of comparison, there are more people in the USA dying from drug overdose every year than deaths during the ten or so years of the war in Vietnam.

Some people believe that people that die from an overdose on drugs feel that it is the victim's fault, that the person was weak, worthless, stupid, or just crazy. This perception is not true. Some also think that drugs are just a problem of the inner city. This perception is also not true. For sure, the youth that overdose are from the suburbs, and they are from prosperous families. Many say that drugs are taking the best and the brightest kids from us long before they can contribute to society. Drugs are no longer the property of the inner city, or of any ethnic group; they are everywhere. Hard Drugs are in your high schools, at your high school parties, on college campuses, in your town, your neighborhood, and even maybe in your home. No one is immune to the threat of addiction. No one.

    This book is divided into separate chapters that deal with certain topics. This first book in the Trilogy is about the reality of what is happening to us, our society, and our future.

Kent I. Phillips
kipphillips46@gmail.com

Section 1

The Origins

The Opioid Crisis

Where Did It Come From?

Our country is "waist deep" in an Opioid addiction crisis. Addiction targets all of America, and the problem is accelerating at a frightening rate. Drug overdoses are no longer part of the "inner city." Overdoses happen to the best families, in rural and suburban communities, and often arrive without notice. The bulk of overdose deaths are usually accompanied by a comment about the victim such as, "I just had no idea!" Almost everyone knows of a victim and the victim's family.

Our society, as discussed in the next chapter, is conditioned to "self medicate" ourselves with aspirin, antibiotics, pain meds, etc. Taking something is the answer to most maladies. Drugs are advertised on television and elsewhere as fantastic "cure alls." So the pathway to Addiction may already be paved. The message to all seems to be, "It's okay to take a drug to help you!"

A negative factor in the USA is the attitude towards marijuana. Marijuana is illegal in the United States by Federal Law. It is a controlled substance. Marijuana is also the number one dollar volume and profit generator for the groups from South of the Border who smuggle drugs into the USA. For years, lots of people have been smoking pot, sometimes in front of their kids. The kids may be warned in school drug education that marijuana is a harmful drug, yet they see their parents smoking joints on the back porch. What these parents are doing is reinforcing an attitude that drugs are okay! Most kids probably have the attitude that, "I can try drugs!" "One time will not hurt me!"

Today, our youth might steal a pain killer from their parent's medicine cabinet and learn what a "high" is all about. True, one time will not hurt you, but it just might flip some kind of a mysterious "switch" in your brain towards further use and abuse. Human brains are not fully developed until about age 22 or so. There is powerful evidence to suggest that using drugs or alcohol during the brain development years, prior to age 22, can lead to future use, abuse, and addiction. No one truly knows why, but somehow the brain starts to crave the euphoria delivered by substances. Young users chart an overwhelming positive statistic of future use and abuse.

Part of the crisis may be that we have set a stage, or at least tacitly approved, using drugs for recreational purposes. At the same time, the Cartels of the Central and South American drug smugglers began to realize that the biggest market for their products was NOT in the inner city, but in the suburbs! They began to focus their distributors on the non-metro areas. What they have found so far is a market that is ready to experiment with drugs. Experimentation, they know, is the first step towards addiction and a growing customer base.

So, one cause of the drug problem in America is an acceptance of self-medication and drug dealers pushing drugs in the suburbs. Combined with these two factors is the fact that the government, the DEA, the FBI, ICE, Homeland, the Coast Guard, Border Security, and local police have failed miserably in reducing the volume of drugs pouring into our nation. With all the resources and money in the world targeted against drug smuggling, the amounts brought into the country have increased, not decreased. The often-mentioned War on Drugs is failing.

Our educational efforts to youth about the dangers of drug use have failed, and our treatment protocols for addicts is failing as well. More on this will be later in this book, but relapse following treatment for hard drugs is well over 90 percent, no matter what any treatment center claims. One of the most debatable aspects of today's treatment failures is the concept of referring to addiction as a "disease." I think the Disease Model of addiction may have been created by Alcoholics Anonymous many years ago. Treatment centers refer to the disease model, saying that addiction itself is a disease. Addiction as a disease has no cure, it is lifelong. When treatment approaches hard drug addiction as a disease, the assumption is that alcohol is somehow similar to drugs like heroin. If we say that the person addicted to is the same as one addicted to heroin, then we can say that they both have a disease and use the same protocols for both in treatment. Assuming that the addiction to alcohol and heroin is the same disease is a tragic mistake. Opioid addiction and alcohol addiction are *not the same disease*. Simply, the lure of relapse for heroin users is significantly more powerful than for alcoholics. Alcoholics *never* glorify getting drunk, or view drinking as a "wonderful thing to do." Heroin addicts will always glorify drug use, and even abuse. Most consider overdose as an acceptable event in the user's lifestyle, and most have been saved from overdose death with an injection of Narcan. Therapy considers both addictions to be the same, as they are both additions. True, they are an addictive "disease," but as unalike as brain cancer is to a sprained ankle. Each requires different treatment. To date, treatment centers supply alcoholics and hard drug addicts with the same protocols. Of course, this treatment approach yields little.

Our crisis is not just due to one single thing. There have been a series of mistakes and failures. Specifically, the key failures are:

1. Youth education programs.
2. Governmental failures to impede illegal importation.
3. Increased volume and penetration of distribution.
4. Lack of youths willingness to report substance existence.
5. Community solidarity in preventing drug distribution and use.
6. Treatment protocols are outdated and unfocused.

So if people ask, "why do we have such a problem?" The answer is complex and is truly a breakdown of our systems. We are now at a point to be less concerned with the "why" or the "how" of the Opioid Epidemic, and we move on to the question of *"what should we do about it now?"* There is no simple answer. It looks like the government with all their powers have failed to protect us. I suppose that the public will have to become more active. The rapid expansion of drug availability in our communities truly has caught us, the police, educational efforts, and the treatment industry, by surprise.

Addiction in our middle schools and high schools is not some strange accident. This population did not just wake up and start using drugs. Amidst all of our six failures as a nation and community, the young people of our nation have been specifically "targeted" for drug use and addiction. Dealers selling cocaine, crack cocaine, meth, and heroin *attack* our youth, since having a young addict is much better from a marketing standpoint than an older addict. All addicts will eventually self-destruct, so younger addicts offer the dealers a longer period to market their products. The drug invasion into our communities is not just coincidental; we have been specifically and successfully attacked.

In summary, our problem is here and growing because of:

1. We are a nation of self-medication. Drugs are okay!
2. The agencies, both national and local, have failed.
3. Drug marketers have shifted their emphasis out of the "inner city."
4. Dealers focus on younger customers.
5. Parents are in denial about drug availability and use.
6. Our youth does not provide us with much information.
7. Drug marketers (Cartels) are very sophisticated and organized.
8. Educational programs and therapies are failing.

American overdose is real and now. In many cases, these kids who overdosed were not saved by a Narcan dose in time. They were unlucky. Overdose is the final event in an addict's life, and it is an American tragedy. I think that the best approach to reversing our addictions in America is to look at the eight causes above and start working on them.

Self-Medication

The Beginning

Let's face it, Americans are simply "pill people." I am not sure when this tradition began, but I think this habit in our culture started developing around the 1950's or so. "Pill popping" has not always been in our nature. Prior to the 1950's, the first place we all went for a cure was what is now called a compound pharmacy. Pharmacies were an apothecary, with pharmacists working behind the counter. Americans did not rush to the doctor as the first stop when we had pain, a cold, a cough, the flu, or a bad headache. If the malady continued, and was not relieved by chicken soup, inhaling steam or some other "home cure," we would have gone to the apothecary, and the pharmacist would whip up a concoction for our relief. I sort of know about this process since my father and his father were both registered pharmacists. Both of them were referred to commonly as "doctor" in the community.

Sometime around this era, the FDA came into its own, and the concept of prescription drugs arrived. I am not sure what role the American Medical Association played in the conversion, but drugs were classified in new ways; some became "prescription only" and the others were deemed "over the counter." Many medications that today we buy regularly off of the shelf in drug stores were classified initially as "prescription only." Enter Big Pharmaceutical companies. Along with the arrival of television came a whole new onslaught of advertising products that were available on the shelf or by prescription. At the same time, the apothecaries were all replaced by DRUG STORES. One drug company advertised Bayer aspirin as being a rapid cure for headaches. Of particular interest was the commercial that advised people, and particularly housewives, to take a "Bayer Break!" The Bayer-Break commercial claimed that when one was feeling stressed on the job or with housework, one should take two aspirins and sit down for a while. The image promoted here was that two aspirin would somehow make the day go "better." I have no idea what the two aspirin were supposed to provide, but the *idea of daily medication began.* Of interest is the appearance of the term "drug store," which, I think, kind of implies that this kind of store provides cure and relief. Realistically, about everything sold off the counter in a drug store will only ease a *symptom* of an ailment, but not the ailment itself.

I am not indicting Bayer as a lone converter of the American habit of medications, only using their efforts as an example of only one company. Today, we have prescription drugs marketed directly to the consumer, direct to the patient. The statements usually are: "if you are taking *this drug, our drug* will work better." The problem with direct advertising is that it really works. Physicians are inundated with requests from their patients to try the new drug instead of the old one. The doctor will probably take the attitude of, "ok, I guess we can try it!" In this case a patient may actually be self-diagnosing. In fact, if we have something like a cold, we immediately start a process of self-diagnosis and self-medication. Personally, I rush to the vitamin cabinet and take Vitamin C, two ibuprofen, and call the doctor for a prescription of antibiotics. You might do the same and think nothing of this process. Many people have almost a pharmacist's vocabulary when it comes to cures. Do not forget that pharma is *big money!*

Okay, I think we can all see how we have come to use drugs and self-medication as a normal process in our culture. We think nothing of "popping" a pill. The concept of taking a pill for relief has influenced our youth. Hydrocodone (Vicodin) is manufactured at the estimated rate of over *forty billion pills per year.* That's $40,000,000,000 individual doses. While this is a world supply, the bulk of prescriptions for this single popular pain killer is filled in the USA. Note this forty billion does *not include* oxycodone, oxycontin, percocet, darvocet, or any of the other *opioid* pain medications prescribed in huge numbers. Just so we are together on the size of this issue, the hydrocodone pills by themselves would be about 125 pills per year for every man, woman, and child in the United States. Wow! And they are all being used by Americans! Here in Arizona, we track closely prescription activity, and in the month of May, 2018, 315,000 prescriptions were written for pain killers. Yes, you read it correctly.

SELF-MEDICATION

Now, let's see how this process might influence our youth, or anyone, to start using harmful substances. First, there are some statements and maybe absolutes that we might consider. Specifically these are:

1. Generally, most substance abusers present with a comorbid condition. This means that they are living with Anxiety, Depression, Personality Disorder, Bipolar, or some other mental illness. We all have Anxiety because it is, in general, a human motivator. If one wakes up late for work, they feel anxiety and start moving quickly. Anxiety is part of living. The young are just starting to learn about it while growing up. One of the continuing shortfalls in drug treatment centers is that mental conditions are not detected in a patient until the abused drug wears off after detox. We treat the users addiction but never identify properly or treat co-existing disorders. The patient leaves with the same mental condition after treatment as they were self-medicating before treatment. This condition may very well be one of the basis for relapse.

2. Adolescents sometimes have a higher than normal anxiety level, as they are physically maturing, learning new things, maturing sexually, self-doubting, over dramatizing, etc. Sometimes these levels are high enough to spawn Depression at low levels. These are normal issues with about all teenagers. They are part of the maturing process. If an adolescent samples some drug, such as alcohol, marijuana, meth, cocaine, a pain pill, or heroin, the worries and concerns about life quickly dissolve. The problem is that alcohol and drugs really work!

3. Availability of substances, and for sure addictive and harmful substances, is prevalent to most youth in our communities. It is easier and cheaper for a minor to obtain an illegal, addictive drug, than it is a six pack of beer. The drug cartels have penetrated to even the smallest of suburban towns. If one thinks that drugs are not available in their little rural town, ask a local emergency room technician about arrivals.

4. False beliefs-today's youth have been conditioned to using a pill to alleviate pain, sorrow, depression, or symptoms. At the same time, they see adults drinking and have come to believe that drugs such as marijuana are harmless. The term "medicinal marijuana" always confuses me, as pot is just another drug, and it is not harmless. Drinking is how most adults deal with daily stressors, so the youth watching

adults drinking, smoking, or taking pills gives them the picture that we should always medicate our physical or mental maladies. Although some find solace in yoga and meditation, they find relief is much quicker and easier if one justs pops a pill. Once they discover how drugs reduce mental and physical pain, most will keep using drugs for the rest of their lives.

So Americans live in a world of medication, and what might be called "pill popping" in the hopes that taking something will provide relief. A person that is already sort of struggling with the world around them, maybe with higher anxiety depression levels than normal, sniffs a very, very, small pinch of heroin, cocaine, or methamphetamine at a party. Sniffing seems innocent enough, and certainly can't be harmful in any serious way, right? This is Correct for most of the population; maybe for 80 percent, sniffing a drug one time is not a serious or hazardous event; but for the other 20 percent, something amazing happens!

The problem with these harmful drugs is simple. *They work very well.* Every worry, feeling of inadequacy, concern, fear, anxiety, stress, and angst disappears in less than a minute. The first experience one has with a substance sometimes can be almost like an awakening, or maybe a birth. A strong and dramatic event this is, with powerful levels of euphoria. Sometimes it leads the individual to ask, "Why have I not done this before?" This is the way to live!" More people than we would like to believe begin a process of regular or intermittent substance use. For many, getting high becomes a regular weekend event. Slowly, the addiction process begins. After a while, getting high on Thursday night or some other day is added to the weekend doses. Every day drug use can, for many, become a regular habit. The addiction process may take months or years; everyone is different. Remember, hard drug use is physiologically addictive. When one uses opioids, meth, or cocaine regularly they *will* become addicted.

Of course, heavier drug use is very expensive, so the addicted person needs daily finance. At this point, the addicted begin to lie, steal, cheat, rob, prostitute, etc. At this point, we are dealing with a fairly desperate, full blown addict.

We will discuss options for each case, and provide suggestions and assessments. Please note though, that when we consider what we have developed in this country, (a "pill popping" culture, stressful lives, and readily available illegal drugs) we can start to look at the addict not as a weak person, or a loser, but as a *victim*.

SELF-MEDICATION

Imagine a teenager, when coming home from school, who sees their mother and father drinking and smoking after work. After a few years of watching them, the teenager develops an attitude that "drinking and smoking must be okay because my parents do it." In a few months, the parents receive a phone call from their child from the police station. The child was "busted" for underage drinking. The parents then say, innocently, that "we just can't understand why our child would do something like this!" Yes, this truly happens all of the time.

So we have sort of conditioned our youth to believe that drinking is part of life, taking pills will make your life better, marijuana is okay to use recreationally, and "doing something once in a while" is *okay*. True, "once in a while" might be okay, but for many adolescents, the "once in a while" will swell up to become a total addiction. In some ways the kids just don't stand a chance. Our culture itself, with the constant emphasis on medications and drugs for making life "better," is a significant factor in the *opioid crisis*.

Hard Drug Statements
Opioid, Meth, and Cocaine

First of all, nothing is new about Heroin. Heroin has been around for decades and abused for decades as well. Most Americans are horrified when they even hear the word, let alone when they discover that this drug is now in widespread distribution and use. YES, it is in your community as well. We all have a rather naive image, perhaps created by some motion pictures, of a heroin addict collapsed in a corner with a hypodermic syringe in some inner city "flophouse." This vision is rather naïve and inaccurate. Today, teenagers have heroin, cocaine, or methamphetamine at parties, and the first experience is euphoric, generated from just "sniffing" the powder. These drugs, thanks to the designs of the Cartels, are everywhere.

Many teenagers are bringing heroin to parties. The kids sniff a little, and in a few seconds, every adolescent issue, anxiety, poor self-image issue, and/or depression, dissolve into a fantastic euphoria. What was invented as a premier pain reliever also works fabulously as a euphoric drug. The youth of our nation might start with a single sniff on Saturday night and slowly expand into daily addictive use. The addiction leads the user into using an intravenous method, because intravenous is the fastest and most powerful method of intake. Heroin addiction is not immediate; it is a process that can take several months or even years.

I know that you might be thinking, "We don't have a problem around here!" And that may be true. When an adult asks their children the big question, "Are there drugs here in school or at parties?" the youth will most likely answer "no!" The reason they will usually say "no" is because if they say "yes" the parent is going to immediately ask a batch of questions like:

"Who is taking them?"
"Have you seen these drugs?"
"Where have you seen them?"
"Are any of your friends taking drugs?"
"Do any of your drug friends come into our house?"
"We have to report these people to the sheriff!"
"I want *you* to take a drug test today!"

So an answer of "yes" might immediately place the child in a hailstorm of adult questions. It is best for them to just say "no." There exists almost a secret society around hard drugs, and few young people want to cross the line of admission and reveal what is really happening. Our attitudes keep us in the dark.

The cartels that produce, distribute, and sell hard drugs altered their marketing targets about five years ago. In the past, the inner city was the place where the hard drugs were sold. About 2012 or so, the marketers began to realize that the big money is NOT in the inner city, but in the middle and upper middle class neighborhoods, as well as the rural communities. The target customer for drugs became under 25 years of age in a nice neighborhood. The more affluent, the better. Generally, wealthier kids have more money and mobility.

Drug availability is widespread and has few restrictions. Certainly, the Federal agencies and the local law enforcement have had no impact in reducing distribution or sales. All of their efforts have resulted in *more drugs nationwide*.

One of the arguments against recreational marijuana on a state level is the fact that the cartel's biggest single product selling to America is Marijuana. No drug is even close to the volume of imported pot, and it has been coming into the country in ever -increasing supply. Well, when recreational marijuana is approved by a state referendum, the drug sellers are instantly robbed of their biggest profit and volume item. I am not naive enough to believe that a dealer selling pot will just "close up and go home" when his product is legalized. No, he will begin offering other stronger, more effective, and maybe more lethal products to the same customer base.

I have had patients relapse here in Phoenix by ordering the product on a web site. The dealer will drive to your home with heroin for sale! I am not sure where this site is on the web, but "dial a drug" is real and happening right now.

Teenagers that use any drugs or alcohol are likely to experiment with heroin. Repeated use leads to physiological addiction in weeks.

Most adolescents face stress from a number of issues while "growing up," including anxiety, self-doubt, depression, social acclimation, physical change, and inferiority. Most of these feelings or challenges are normal; sometimes they are at very strong levels. One tiny sniff of a hard drug, such as an opioid, meth or cocaine, and all of these mental issues dissolve into euphoria, starting a very tempting base of further use. One in ten become addicts or abusers.

Treatment centers utilize protocols addressing the issues of an addicted world of three to five years ago, and their protocols are ineffective in treating the "H patient." This could be due to the fact that most protocols became "approved" by counseling professionals during a different point in time. The bulk of current treatments are ineffective and are geared more to the alcoholic patient rather than effectively treating the hard drug addict. Treatment for heroin use is failing, and the relapse rate following treatment is over 90 percent, no matter what the center claims. The image of a youth returning to a "normal" life after thirty to ninety days in a treatment center is a total falsehood. Treatment protocols usually are based upon group meetings such as AA or NA, role-playing, cognitive behavioral therapy, and other "behavioral altering" methodologies. Frankly, talking and thinking is just not powerful enough to counteract the lure of heroin, particularly after the patient has detoxed.

Compared to alcoholics, H patients seem to have a very low interest in remaining sober. Often "H" patients or Hard Drug Patients glorify and experience euphoric recall influenced by their history and experience. After detox, the pleasant memories seem often to outweigh the challenging lifestyle of the addict. Negative memories seem to melt, yet the "lure" of being high remain. Alcoholics, on the other hand, seldom would state that drinking was "wonderful." "H" patients are unique in this manner. They *want* to get high.

Defiance, usually represented powerfully by a lack of *will* to remain sober, is the core issue in transitioning to a true long term recovery. The second issue is *boredom*. Few if any treatment centers measure these two complex conditions and none have developed adequate treatment protocols of treatment.

Is this lack of *will* the result of heroin addiction? Is the lure and attraction and memories of heroin use overpowering that will, or is the patient simply void of will power to begin with? This is unknown, unmeasured, and in some ways, not important in an adequate and designed protocol. Treatment should *develop willpower*.

Treatment looks at traditional psychological "causes" of addiction problems, such as trauma, childhood, events, and family structure, assuming that addiction is a "family problem" etc.; it may be that none of these issues are really at play in reckless heroin use at all. Heroin has its own game of use and abuse, mental and physiological addiction. Our youth may begin using just for "fun," and then abuse in addictive fashion due to the nature of the drug itself. Simply put, hard drugs provide an immense relief to any mental condition. *They work.*

If Treatment is treating these "causes" and not spawning the *will* to recover, treatment time and energy is wasted. With any addiction, the criteria for treatment success is solely determined by the desire of the patient to change. The fact that current treatment modalities are somewhat ineffective, as evidenced by the pitiful recovery statistics of treatment centers, makes the situation worse, not better.

Heroin, Cocaine and Methamphetamines seem to be too powerful for today's treatment protocols. So far, we just can't outsmart hard drug addiction.

On the horizon, however, are some new treatment methodologies. A promising one is the concept of Medically Assisted Treatment, combining medications that prevent euphoric responses from alcohol or opioids with therapy. These drugs will not allow the user of opioids or alcohol to attain any kind of "high." They block the receptors. If the patient has even a slight will to change and stays on the medication and therapy, the preliminary "cure rates" are positive. Medically Assisted Therapy (MAT) might be the wave of the future, as opposed to standard treatment. The patient can stay on the job, stay in school, or stay at home for the entire treatment period. They remain productive in the world during the process.

One thing about these hard drugs: Kids that get "hooked" are victims of our failures to protect them. Most young people who become addicted or reliant upon substances are the best and the brightest. There is always an opinion in a community that a person falling into a cycle of addiction is a "bum" or "worthless." Nothing could be further than the truth. In many cases, addicted youth find great solace from family issues, relationship problems, clinical level anxiety and/or depression, or just plain sadness. Realize that more than half of our kids are from families that are in crisis with divorce, addiction, death, or financial struggles. When these struggling kids have that first experience of alcohol, marijuana, cocaine, meth, heroin, or designer drugs (Ecstasy), all of these "problems" go away. A brief period of euphoria is experienced. In addition, most people under 30 or so seem to host a belief that most of these drugs, even the illicit powerful ones, are harmless when used occasionally. From a physical standpoint, maybe they are harmless, but to about one in ten people who might have a propensity towards addiction, they can initiate a path towards regular use, abuse, and addiction. Addiction is a process that affects one in ten; it knows no boundaries, demographics, or social levels. The fact that drugs are everywhere in the USA enhances the trap of addiction that is just quietly waiting to strike the innocent. One single casual use can result in long term addiction, and no one knows exactly who will be the victim.

The Progression

It may be that you are reading this book because you want to learn more about Opioid addiction and have an afflicted loved one. If so, this chapter is to help and reassure you that addiction follows a regular pattern, and few addicts have unique experiences. There are hundreds of thousands, maybe millions, addicted today. You are not alone. You may feel at your wits-end and that you are all alone, but what you are experiencing is happening nationwide.

Addiction to Opioids follows a consistent pattern. The initial point of exposure is from pain pills prescribed or taken (stolen) from someone's medicine cabinet. This is a very common introduction. The only other point of exposure is from a "friend" that uses other drugs, such as meth or cocaine, and the addict is already addicted to something else. The Opioid, in this case, is a new drug experience.

Opioids offer a very special type of euphoria, and the stronger the Opioid (heroin), the greater the euphoria. A person who begins their experience with a pain pill, like Oxycodone, or Vicodin, will progress in their use level. The single pain pill becomes two, then three, then four, etc. Eventually, prescriptions will run out, and the cravings propel the user to find drugs on the street. Because the street drugs are more expensive, the user will learn that by breaking the pills, adding water, and injecting them, the effect is more powerful than heroin. Remember, heroin is easier to obtain and cheaper than a six pack of craft brewed beer (particularly for a minor). The user that is offered heroin from a friend will immediately enjoy the euphoric power of heroin. Heroin seems to be the top euphoric on sale.

The next step in the progression is the need for larger and larger doses to reach the same euphoric stage, since the body slowly adapts to the dose levels. Coinciding with the increased dosage is the need for more and more money. The need for finance will more than likely lead the addict to begin a life of obtaining funds by lying, borrowing, stealing, prostitution, relationships for the purposes of obtaining money, etc. Normally, the criminal activity leads to legal problems and jail sentences. Often the user becomes a dealer to support the habit.

One problem with a jail sentence is that it is usually a felony conviction, tarnishing the record of the addict forever. A second problem is that few penal institutions offer any therapy or counseling for addiction. The addict enters jail an addict, has to detox, serves the time, then is released to immediately relapse.

Often, the released addict will overdose, since the drugs are stronger today, and they will take too large of a dose. These overdoses lead to death if they are not administered a Narcan injection in time.

This chapter is for those who are suffering a life with a loved one who is addicted. Please understand that almost all addicts tend to follow this general progression. The development of the addicted is common, documented, and "normal."

More often than not, this will be the progression of your loved one as well. They are at some point along this continuum, and they will follow this path unless interrupted. Remember the addict has to decide to recover. Any effort to help them will fail, unless they have made a true decision to recover. The heartbreaking fact is that we never know if the user is being sincere or not, and I think it is safe to say that most of the time, they are not. When their lives hit bottom, and they face homelessness, etc. they will say anything and do anything to buy time and drugs. Anything.

The Progression:

1. Person comes to believe that drugs are harmless if sampled or used in small quantities.
2. Sampled drugs provide a life-changing euphoria.
3. The drug experience is repeated on the weekends.
4. The drug is used more than on the weekends and drifts into daily consumption.
5. Individual becomes physiologically and psychologically dependent and addicted.

6. Individual changes lifestyle toward obtaining funds to obtain an ever-increasing amount of the substance.
7. Addict experiences legal problems, institutions, treatment centers, and detox.
8. Individual relapses and overdoses, sometimes with lethal consequences.

I truly wish that this progression were not accurate, but unfortunately it is the normal path of the hard drug addict. These eight events are going to happen in about every addict's life. There are very few exceptions.

There is no statistical data to support these conclusions, but I think most addiction therapists would tell you that:

1. Most hard drug addicts started by smoking pot..
2. Most hard drug addicts are cigarette or vape smokers.
3. Most hard drug addicts remember the day they first used a needle.
4. Most hard drug addicts started using hard drugs first at a party.
5. Most hard drug addicts also have a co-occurring disorder that they are "self-medicating."
6. Most hard drug addicts find treatment a silly exercise.

So, in summary, addiction is not a mystery. It is known, progressive, predictable, and consistent. For our youth, hard drugs are basically right in front of them at parties, and at home as well. What was first just a temptation becomes a progressive illness with few, if any, treatments that are successful. Addiction has TWO outcomes; Recovery, or Institutions and Death.

The Substance Nation

In America, there is a rising new "nation within a nation." Generation Q, the quiet generation, born between 1998 and 2018. The Substance Nation thriving within this generation is unique and separate, with different cultural aspects, values, languages, and behaviors. In essence, this nation is not a part of the mainstream American culture. They accept and glorify the use of substances, such as heroin. They contribute little to society, and in many cases, damage it. Predators (drug dealers) look at this population segment as a market in which to sell illegal substances. Evidence suggests that this Nation is bigger than estimated, and it is growing! Most Americans mistakenly believe that this culture is not in their high schools, towns, or on their street. They are wrong. The problem is everywhere! If you have a young addict in your home, they are more than likely a part of this growing societal segment. Some of the unique cultural aspects of this emerging group are:

1. Overdose is a part of life (combat platoon mentality). Members of this culture are addicted to hard drugs, unmindful of the growing number of deaths by overdose. They seem to accept the possibility of overdose and overdose death with an extreme lightness. Some have exclaimed, when treated with Narcan following a deadly overdose, that they "did not" want to be revived. This is similar to "combat platoon" members, accepting that some will die.

2. Getting high is synonymous with fun; getting very high is more fun. A cultural aspect of this group is a unified interpretation of hard drug or opiate use as being a "party time." They reflect on drug use, in a group, as being an exciting party affair. In reality, heroin or other opiate injectables usually render the recipient prone and half asleep,

not dancing joyously at some lively festival. They would have probably been lying somewhere in the corner sort of dazed and mostly unconscious.

3. Good times are often associated with hard drug use. While using and addicted, the addict is living a nightmare life of cycles: finding money to buy drugs and buying drugs to support a daily habit. However, once citizens from this culture have detoxed for a week or so, their memories of being high seem to suppress any of the negative thoughts associated with active using. By comparison, after many years of being in Alcoholics Anonymous meetings, I have never heard anyone say, "I used to drink ten beers and two fifths of Vodka every day, and I just felt great!" Alcoholics may have "cravings," but I have never heard anyone in recovery speak positively about being drunk or hung-over. Addicts can quickly enter a euphoric recall state and exclaim that "being high" is wonderful. Often they will believe that no advisor, counselor, or family member can understand the addict because they have never tried heroin. The horror of the addict's previous lifestyle seems to drift from consciousness after treatment detox. Getting high starts to sound good again. Real good.

4. Unique language and slang. The Substance Nation uses a different language. Yes, it is a series of slang terms, but there is an additional "understanding" between members and unique and differentiated meanings of some words. As an example, "Police", "Jail", "Treatment," and "Juvee" are synonymous with "vacation." This language also contains many "slang" expressions for hundreds of drug related terms.

5. Going to jail is part of life, and often a "badge of honor"—jail is just part of living. I have had patients that have been indicted for armed robbery at age 15, served jail time, and are on ten-year probations. They often laugh when speaking of their legal misadventures, and to some may be part of what might be called "bragging rights" later in life. In the Substance Nation, legal problems seem to add credence to the "life."

6. Male/female relationships are "value added" and purpose driven (not love). More often than not, male addicts find themselves living with female addicts. This is not a relationship of love, but one of almost tribal reverence to obtaining and using drugs daily. Sex, childbearing, staying high, and prostitution is okay, as long as the couple is

continuing to "score" funds to support the daily drug habit. These are relationships of convenience and are aimed towards a single goal.

7. Days are spent in "capturing" money for drugs. Obtaining hard drugs is the daily goal and motivator. To that end, stealing, robbing, shoplifting, and lying is accepted and part of the process deemed "normal" in this culture. Even grandma's beautiful wedding ring is fair game to take to the pawn shop and obtain money for drugs. Somehow the addicts seem to feel that either "people (even family) has so much money they won't miss this" or "hey, no one realizes how much I need this money!" Most of the time, the parents notice cash or valuables disappearing, but are too naive or in denial to pursue.

    Since addicts always need money to buy drugs, they will often resort to daily shoplifting to provide bare essentials. Stealing food, cosmetics, clothing, and other consumables is a daily adventure. Stealing these items leaves more money for drugs.

8. Illegitimate children are part of life. It is not unusual for culture members to have one or more children, sometimes from a drug using female companion. Often the father is unclear how the pregnancy happened. Today's Neonatal Intensive Care Units have an "epidemic" of addicted newborns. Being born addicted is not often fatal, but the babies have to go through a detox procedure that is rather unpleasant. Odd that while the baby is detoxing, the parents are on the street using.

9. Prostitution is normal, if not always admitted (both sexes). While most Substance Nation members will deny illicit sexual activities, most have been involved in prostitution to obtain drug money. While sex is kept private in discussions, almost all addicts, if in the drug game long enough, have sold their bodies for sex.

10. Going to treatment is like a vacation, with food and lodging provided. A constant and ever-present enabling thought is that if I relapse after treatment, I can always go to another center here in this state, or on the beach in California or Florida.

    "Another treatment center is probably the worst thing that can happen to me," is often on the addict's mind. Most often, the addict feels that they can always "squeeze" some support from parents or relatives. Frankly, the motivation of addicts to obtain finance and support from others seems to have been developed into an "art form" by most.

Knowing that there can always be another treatment center on the horizon completely removes the motivation to engage in a current treatment regimen, twelve step work, or long-term sobriety. No published statistics exist, but a normal cycle might be:

- Go to treatment for 90 days.
- During treatment, pose as someone truly making progress in recovery. Stay as long as you can in treatment housing and support.
- Get a job and an apartment at end of treatment.
- Relapse within about one to six weeks after release from treatment. Enter another treatment center.
- Repeat.

I have had patients that are 24 years old, have been using heroin since age 14, and have had almost ten full years of what is called "treatment hopping." So ten years, off and on, of drug use, some jail, and perhaps a dozen different treatment centers. Honestly, these "experts" seem to know more about treatment activities than most of the counselors. And while the patients have "knowledge" of the tips, tools, and techniques used in treatment, they did not impact them positively. Somehow, they have just missed the point of any exercise.

11. Felony arrests are the rule, not the exception. This can be stealing, dealing, breaking and entering, felony drug arrests, prostitution, concealed weapons, drug paraphernalia, possession. Depending on the state and the age of the offender, these felonies can carry some jail time, along with long term probation, monitored by a probation officer.

12. Substance Nation members feel at ease with one another, and ill-at-ease with others outside the culture. There seems to be some quiet acceptance and fellowship among this culture. Many of the patients may know each other from the past, being in the same treatment center, juvenile detention, or jail. Inside the culture, there seems to be a communion of trust, loyalty, and commitment to other members. As an example, residents in a treatment center, if visited by a former resident who stops by to sell drugs, will seldom report this violation

to staff. There seems to be no understanding that this visitor, who brought drugs into the living environment, is hurting the residents. Never will the residents affected report this "invasion" to staff. There always exists a "we" and "them" separation. While staff members may be ex-addicts, few if any will be part of this new Substance Nation, so they will never be privy to the sub-currents in the "nation."

13. Jobs are bottom level due to felony or arrest records and are much less pleasant than dealing drugs. There seems to be a tendency to seek jobs of lower level with very little sense of advancement. No sense of commitment or loyalty to the hiring company exists. There is a "take it or leave it" attitude with these basic jobs. It is almost as if the addict does not want to be involved in something that might attract his or her or interest him or her beyond a basic paycheck. Every job is temporary.

14. Culture members under twenty-one years of age can obtain hard drugs more easily and for less money than alcohol. More than likely, your community has reached a level of having Black Tar heroin available. Young culture members state that it is easier to buy heroin than beer, and the cost is about the same. Availability is never a problem. Today the "dial a dealer" system exists, so the drugs are brought to you wherever you can meet the dealer. Here in Phoenix, there is a website to contact dealers to have drugs delivered to your door.

15. Hepatitis C is normal in this culture due to sharing of needles. The popular thinking is that this malady, or any others, can pretty much be cured with various medications. The only real fear, and it usually is tested for entering treatment, is HIV. There is actually a great sigh of relief when a patient's test comes back positive for Hepatitis and negative for HIV/Aids. Hep C is considered something to have treated in the "future, sometime."

16. Neither friends, nor friendships, nor love, exist here, asrelationships are centered upon obtaining drugs and using them. Father, mother, aunts and uncles, friends, brother, sister, NO ONE has any influence compared to the lure and power of drugs. Drugs have the complete power over the addict's emotions. Statements of "I love you" might really mean, "Will you consider giving me money if I ask?"

17. Stealing money from friends, parents, and relatives is accepted. Stealing from a store is not only accepted, it is almost a challenge of sorts. Robbing stores is definitely "okay." The concept of taking from a

company or corporation takes on an almost religious crusade, and the ability to "beat the man" adds to an individual's status.

18. A cycle of guilt and shame is self-perpetuating. Addicts steal, feel guilty, mask the guilt with drugs, etc. Guilt and Shame build up in the user to very high levels; the longer the "use cycle," the longer the "drugging cycle," the greater the angst within the patient. Feelings exist way below the surface and are not revealed in the treatment process without intensive counseling. Members of the Substance Nation have drowned their inner feelings for years with drugs and alcohol. Feelings are suppressed but continue to generate high anxiety levels; remember always that drugs and alcohol perfectly self-medicate anxiety on a short-term basis. They work.

19. Younger members enter this culture each year; the average age is declining! Society is rather blind to these statistics, and maybe some communities feel they are unscathed by the hard drug problem. Some parents just want to deny that a problem exists in their city, neighborhood, Junior High School, or family. The group on the higher edge of the Nation was probably born in the mid-nineties, so in their early to mid—twenties. Their use or sampling initiation probably was around the year 2010 or so. By the same token, around the beginning of that same decade, kids that were 12 or so began to experiment. Today, this group is anywhere from age 15 to age 20. So, the using group is getting younger, and it is building to a higher level of users. Before you say to yourself that "we don't have a problem here," check out your local ER rooms and find out how many overdoses come in each week. Compare it to the same week of last year.

    What you will find is that overdoses have increased two to five-fold, which probably means the use level is up two to five-fold. Note again that these overdoses are *not* in the inner city anymore. They are local.

20. Standard psychological treatment protocols will *not* work with this culture! I have already mentioned that treatment centers do not work, and that the patients with strong treatment center experience already know all the protocols in advance. In the center, this creates an extreme level of boredom and a very strange dependence on expectations for the center to "fix the addict" rather than the addict learning to "fix himself or herself." One of the reasons that the centers do not

work well is that they fail to recognize they are treating not only an addict, but also a person from a different *culture*, a different *nation*.

21. Feelings of hopelessness are self-medicated daily. Yes, living on the street addicted to hard drugs such as heroin or meth is probably not fun. Most people using feel extremely hopeless and worthless; they have failed at almost everything. All of these negative feelings, self-assessments, behavior, sadness, lack of relationships, loss of family contact, and so on all disappear upon injection of the drug. The problem is "drugs work" until they wear off. All the shame, guilt, anxiety, and fear dissolve in seconds with a drug.

22. Therapy with this group has dismal results; almost all relapse. There are all price ranges in treatment centers, from government supported facilities to expensive, $60,000-a-month operations. All of them will claim some sort of success. With this NATION, their success rate is dismal, to the point of being non-existent. I spent a couple of months at one of the most premier treatment centers in the world. Of the probably 40 people I knew there, I have personal knowledge of 37 relapsing that I know of. That would represent some 90 percent of patients relapsing. As I say, there are a lot of claims about success rates, but if you are curious, ask the center you are considering what is their "cure rate" with patients under twenty-five years of age.

    Most members of the nation have had several treatment experiences, sometimes starting as young as 14 years old. They have, in some cases, been in five to ten treatment centers, and have no true desire to remain sober. These patients have seen about every attempt to help them in therapy. The most important to a Substance Nation member is not the protocols or treatment, but the fact that they have a bed and meals. Treatment, oddly, is like a hotel to them.

    One of the key reasons to recognize and understand treatment failures is that a key component of training therapists is recognizing and understanding the cultural differences of the patient. Schooling trains therapists for African American, Hispanic, Native American, and Oriental cultures, but does not even recognize the uniqueness of the Substance Nation. We are not trained to communicate with them nor understand their lifestyles.

23. Defiance is a byword for this culture's lifestyle. All addicts are defiant. There are actually tests available to evaluate children less than

ten years of age, ranking their defiance levels as a predictor for future addiction possibilities. I am not sure what a parent would change, if, for instance, their child ranked high in defiance. Most parents can already see defiance in their kids when young, but what are they supposed to do to protect them? Maybe we should keep them in the woods or something. It could be that "home schooling parents" are a move to isolate the kids from bad influences. I have had some experience with kids that were schooled at home and they seemed far ahead of other children in their age group. Defiance seems to be a strange fuel and motivator for members of the Substance Nation. In many cases, it is a tremendous "block" to treatment engagement, and is very detrimental to recovery. Defiance enables the addict to remain in true denial during treatment and after.

24. Federal efforts to thwart drug sale and use have never been effective. If we ever begin to feel a certain power in being a parent, and that we can have an impact on drug use in school, consider these facts about the problem. The FBI, the DEA, ICE, the Navy, the Army, and the Coast Guard are all in the business of fighting drugs coming into the USA illegally. So far, all of the power of these groups has had almost no impact on drugs coming into the country or manufactured here (Meth). *No impact.* The Substance Nation supports these activities by buying the product, promoting the import, growth, and volume. The cartels that supply substances to the Nation are much more sophisticated and organized than big Pharmaceutical companies, and just as big.

    I believe that since the government and local law enforcement has failed to protect us that we may have to develop "action teams" in our local communities. Engaging our youth to participate, to stop drug dealing in our community. Local action and courage will be needed here.

25. Kids entering the Nation have an impact on, and contribute to, the destruction of the American Family. There is a separate chapter in the *Killing Family* called "Family Dynamics." To summarize, the emerging addict in the family steals the show and resources, and creates jealousy in the other siblings; the addict causes divorce, chaos, and strife.

26. Acculturation in this nation is not time sensitive; it is determined by type and frequency of drug use—some kids start with pot and alcohol

and painkillers and slowly enter the culture. Secretly, they will begin to use harder drugs, with heroin being the general end result. At the point where the child starts using heroin or meth daily, they are part of this secret NATION. This process can happen in a couple of weeks, a couple of months, or a couple of years.

27. The groups and cartels that supply this nation with substances are not just gangs of "crazy Latinos," they are well disciplined, organized production and distribution machines dealing with illicit substances. Their organizations are some of the most sophisticated structures of manufacturing, illegal exporting, distribution and cash return in the world. Compare these cartels to a company like Upjohn or Eli Lilly and Co. Imagine these magnificent companies, maybe the most successful of all time, if they had to bring all their medicines into this country illegally, distribute it outside of the physician and Drug channel, and then return the cash from every sale illegally back across the border. This comparison should clearly indicate to all at what level the cartels operate! Rather frightening, isn't it?

28. The cartels have developed a well-oiled manufacturing, distribution, marketing, and sales organization. Black Tar Heroin, for example, is all coming from Mexico. Once across the border, it is distributed to the local dealers that service the addicts. Usually, there are two dealers in a car with a modest amount of Heroin or other drugs with them. If arrested, the quantities they carry with them generally will yield a short time in jail, or even probation. The dealers realize that prison may well be a part of the job.

29. The Nation is targeted for growth in substance consumption, with new users welcome—Overdose deaths are more than made up by targeted new users. The dealer networks target communities by offering lower priced goods to create a basic user base, grow it, and then move prices up. If you believe that the Nation is not developing in your neighborhood, you are probably somewhere in the beginning development stages. It is there; it is just quiet right now.

30. Illegitimate children are often raised by drug users, and will probably grow up to add more addicts to the Nation. No one is sure whether a propensity for drug use is inherited or arrives via the culture. Statistics clearly show that there is a high level of use among children of addicts and alcoholics. Many of the members of the Nation have parents that

smoke pot, drink alcohol to access, or use hard drugs. The message the young people of these families receive is, "it's okay to use drugs." Imagine being raised by users, and try to picture a child not following their parents into addiction.

31. Arrests, juvenile incarceration, or police activity has no impact on the culture at all—some communities have attempted to "arrest their way" out of drug use. This posture fails miserably, and sometimes places teenagers in very risky prison environments. Generally, this "arrest approach" creates an even worse environment in the long run.

This Substance Nation is not hypothetical; it is real, in great strength and growing. The dwellers are not restricted to urban areas, low income, ghettos, or racial groups. The NATION is in your neighborhood, in your town, your high school, and your house. The treatment world is going to have to understand that dealing with this secret, growing culture requires using prevention, enforcement, and treatment; we need to adjust our tips, tools, and techniques to the culture. The systems will have to change, to adapt, and quickly. I believe that most treatment modalities in place are geared towards alcoholics and *not* hard drug addicts. Even the Twelve Steps of AA were always addressing the alcoholic, and has been "adapted" to relate to others in Narcotics Anonymous, Heroin Anonymous, etc.

Treatment centers fail to understand they are treating a unique, growing culture, the Substance Nation, and are also applying protocols that have been used to treat alcoholics. Frankly, these protocols simply are not working effectively to treat and help members of the Nation.

Section 2

How Bad Is It?

The Opioid Crisis

How Bad Is It?

As I mentioned in the introduction, the Center for Disease Control in Atlanta, Georgia, estimates the death by overdose tally to be about 150 Americans per day. This number would project to be about 60,000 annually. This number is understated, due to the fact that it is based on reports from Emergency Rooms and Medical facilities. Not all overdose deaths are recognized as such. Many families do not want this diagnosis of a deceased loved one and want to hide the truth. Often these overdose deaths are registered as a "heart attack" or "pulmonary embolism." The crisis exists because overdose drug deaths are increasing monthly. There will be new numbers issued in a few weeks. Most of these deaths are young people under thirty.

First responders inject overdosed (almost dead) patients with Narcan, reversing the opioid effects. Apparently, no solid data exists on how many potential overdose deaths are reversed by Narcan (Naloxone), but the small injectable medicines are in the hands of just about every fire department, emergency service, policemen, and many households and treatment facilities. Last year, over $240 million dollars of Naloxone was sold in the USA! In Arizona, there have been about 1,500 drug overdose deaths in the last twelve months, and almost *six thousand* doses of Narcan administered. We have about four deaths a day from drugs, and we would probably have *twenty-two* deaths without the Narcan injections. Arizona is a small state, with only six million residents.

In American prisons today there are about 1.5 million incarcerated. Of these, 65 to 85 percent were under the influence of drugs and/or alcohol at the time they committed a crime. Many were fully addicted to injectable drugs like heroin. Once released from prison, the odds of relapsing on an opioid, overdosing, and dying are very high. Note also that 46 of the 50 states offer little to no treatment for addiction in their prisons. The practice that communities should be "tough on drugs" is very ineffective. We arrest someone, send them to jail, and they get no drug treatment. Today's drug dealers only carry small quantities and often have great lawyers. If we send addicts to jail, they probably can obtain drugs in prison, or will immediately relapse upon release. Jail is no solution.

The opioid user usually starts with a prescription of oxycodone, becomes quickly addicted, then runs out of pill supply. They quickly learn that they can buy street pills, although these pills are much more expensive. The next step is that the addict learns that quartering the pill, adding liquid and injecting, provides a cheaper and more powerful effect. Now the addict has entered a new level in his drug taking—intravenous injections. The next, and maybe final step, is injecting street heroin. This cycle is common, increasing in numbers every year, and is *not* centered in low income areas, the uneducated, or inner cities. Opioid addiction, overdoses, and death know no boundaries. Opioid addiction is in every town, city, state, and region in America.

One of the aspects of opioid addiction is that hundreds of thousands of Americans can be using these drugs, be addicted, and yet function normally in their daily lives. I have had patients that were using heroin daily that worked very dangerous jobs for five or ten years under the influence. Some patients were operating heavy construction equipment, or even working in the construction of high rise buildings in downtown New York City. The idea of walking on a narrow steel beam fifty stories above the Earth, stoned on heroin, seems a little risky and frightening to me, but it is much more common than you think.

The University of Michigan conducts alcohol surveys in hundreds of middle schools and high schools across the land. The most recent data suggests that about 80 percent of high school seniors have experimented with drugs, and about 25 percent are using regularly. This data suggests that our youth have a very casual view of drug use. Many believe that drugs such as marijuana are harmless, and compared to their parents' consumption of alcohol, are better for you. This attitude is frightening to me and indicates that our school drug education systems in place are not working. The data that the University of Michigan survey relies upon is obtained by student reports. When I see data of this type, I am always a little skeptical because the hard drug user may not truly report accurately. They would be suspicious of reporting the truth about heroin.

I do not believe that any illicit drug, alcohol, or nicotine can possibly be considered as a positive alternative to anything. Alcohol and nicotine, both fully legal and accessible in most communities, are *the two biggest health and wellness issues* in the USA. We all know that smoking cigarettes is suspected to cause lung and other lethal diseases, and alcohol can cause colon cancer, breast cancer, liver and pancreatic cancer, and a host of other diseases. Another fact is that the bulk of traffic accidents are caused by intoxicated drivers. It is ridiculous to believe that alcohol and drugs are harmless to humans.

This book is not intended to be a crusade, and I know it will not reduce the level of drug or alcohol use in our nation. The true and real purpose of this publication is to fire a warning shot! Unless some remedy is implemented soon, the number of users and overdose deaths is going to skyrocket.

Using a statistical linear regression on the growth of opioid deaths by overdose, the number will explode in the next five years to hundreds of thousands annually. Please keep in mind that the overdose is the final event in a journey of use, abuse, and addiction, and that medical people, teachers, law enforcement, and some fire departments are equipped with an injectable Narcan that can reverse the overdose symptoms. If administered to a patient that is still alive, the opioid overdose effect is reversed in minutes. Even with this miracle, this lifesaving drug on hand, the overdose deaths continue to increase dramatically every year. The reason that overdoses increase, by the way, is obvious. More and more people are using Opioids.

The National Institute on Drug Abuse surveyed 68,000 high school students. Of these students, over 10 percent reported non-medical opioid use, and 1.2 percent reported "trying" heroin. This may not be too alarming, but if you go to a high school graduation, note that about one out of ten have used opioids, have experienced the euphoria generated by the drug, and had *no* medical reason for the dosage. The reason they used the opioid was to get high! Remember also that these statistics are developed from students *reporting* their drug use, and they may be dramatically understated if students are reluctant to report accurately. I would think that most respondents here would be a little reluctant to reveal their "drug secrets" on a survey. The real number of users might be much, much greater.

Youthful experimentation at these high levels indicate that the problem of the opioid crisis is *just getting started*. If the growth continues, Opioid use and addiction may very well be the number-one health problem in America.

A fact to consider is that the drug Hydrocodone (Vicodin) is manufactured at a level of 40 billion pills per year. Yes, 40 *billion*. Most of these are used in the USA. Hydrocodone is widely prescribed, contains codeine, and is addictive. This drug is prescribed for pain for many purposes, especially following surgery or an accident. Millions are prescribed this drug for "back pain," and it is highly effective. Recently, the law was altered to restrict prescription quantities and refills. These laws will prevent the patient who is using the drug regularly from buying any large quantities or refills that are "phoned in" by a physician's office. While intended to reduce opioid addiction, these restrictions will not have an impact on most users, but some may be influenced to buy illegal and illicit street drugs, such as other forms of opioids. Street drugs are expensive and soon, the addicted will learn that injecting opioids is the most effective and cheapest way to dose. So they advance from taking a pill to injecting.

These new laws may create more problems than they solve. One of the emerging and ongoing problems with buying street drugs, especially of heroin -level power, is that often drugs such as Fentanyl are added to the substance to increase its power. Fentanyl is a synthetic opioid. Not derived from the poppy flower, it is cheaply manufactured right across the border in Mexico and is a hundred times more powerful than heroin. Fentanyl is a killer drug on the street.

While this progression from a pain medication to dangerous street heroin or other drugs might seem unusual to you, I assure you that it is very common. Addiction can happen to anyone, sometimes occurring without the knowledge of the patient. When one discovers that they have a big problem is when they stop taking the long used prescription opioid, such as Oxycontin or Vicodin and they enter into detox. At this point, the user will do just about anything to end their discomfort. Taking the drug quickly ends the discomfort. Addiction does not care if you are in Middle School, High School, College, are aHousewife, Businessman, Athlete, Homeless, or whatever; Addiction does not discriminate. Today, buying street opioids is a common occurrence, and drugs are absolutely, definitely in small town America as well as the big cities. In fact some of the biggest community problems with drugs are in the local, small towns. If you ask your kids, most will tell you that "we do not have a drug problem in our school." While this would be nice, this statement is either a falsehood, or the child is totally out of high school society. Drugs are everywhere.

One of the most alarming facts is the mistaken assumptions among youth that drugs are not harmful. I do not know if this comes from the "recreational marijuana" craze or not, but experimenting with most drugs is considered to be part of youth culture. The parties that I went to when I was young might have some beer, wine, or vodka as a temptation. Today, black tar heroin, china white heroin, cocaine, or methamphetamines will be available for sampling. True, one little sniff of heroin will yield an overwhelming euphoria that dissolves anyone's anxieties. I suppose one time may not be harmful if tried *once*. The reality is, however, that about one in ten will return to this same drug again. Each time one uses, the dosage may have to be a little bit more to attain the "first time" level of euphoria. Using once, on Saturday night, can become an everyday habit. The sniffing becomes injecting, and then the victim is fully addicted. With this terrifying progression, one must conclude that "sampling" a drug *is harmful*. In fact, it could be *lethal*.

Maybe the most chilling aspect of drugs in America is the fact that in reality, all the government efforts, the billions of dollars spent, the attempts at educating our youth, all the police, sheriffs and state police, have had little effect on reducing the flow of drugs. In fact, there are more drugs now than ever before, and the availability is everywhere. Our society is failing to protect us.

There are few sadder things in my practice than when a mother is challenged with an addicted child. Truly they experience a feeling of loss, abandonment, and helplessness that is unparalleled. More will be discussed about this in Book Three, *Killing Family*.

The Clinical Side

Another aspect of the Opioid Epidemic are the problems that patients addicted to opioids and other hard drugs create in therapy sessions. Hard drug addicts in treatment are the most difficult to reach and are seldom touched by any therapeutic attempt. During inpatient treatment, the patient is isolated from the outside world, and drugs are not available for use. The patient arrives in treatment and experiences detox. The detox usually lasts for seven to ten days and is the first hurdle in recovery. Usually medications are given such as Suboxone, or benzodiazapines to lessen the discomfort of detox.

During this period, the suffering addict is in pretty bad shape physically and mentally. Almost all of them have Hepatitis C from needle contamination and sharing. Almost all of them are rather disheveled from street life. Detox is not usually very comfortable, and most patients just want to stay in bed and sleep if they can. At this point in treatment, the patient is very receptive to any kind of help, and they are frightened about the physical and mental condition they have reached during their addiction. More often than not, the patient has experienced treatment in the past.

Near the end of detox, the patient begins full force therapy and education. They experience group sessions, one on one sessions, yoga, relaxation, anger management, trauma therapy, 12 step programs, role playing, process group, educational groups, EMDR sessions, and a host of other protocols. The first few weeks of therapy, the addict is very compliant, and there is a positive receptivity to what might be called "the cure."

After about ten days to two weeks in treatment, something happens.. The patient begins to feel the lure of getting high on heroin again. Somehow, this lure, or attraction, seems to block from memory the horrors of addiction, street life, stealing, prostitution, overdoses and death. In sessions, discussion of using their drug of choice seems to generate a fantasy euphoric feeling that ignores the condition that brought them into treatment. The drug lure is very powerful, and the idea of getting high again seems to be good idea. The addict begins to believe that they can "control" drug use, and could get high "one more time."

Once the addict enters this euphoric recall mode, they have, in effect, mentally left therapy. They begin to hate being in sessions or being involved in any treatment protocols. They will say things like, "I am tired of doing these same things over and over again" and "Twelve step stuff won't work for me!"

In group sessions, they will appear distant and unengaged, and sometimes are disruptive to the treatment process. If the patient is under thirty years of age, the odds are that they have been in other treatment programs before, so most of what happens is a repeat of the past, and these young patients are often unengaged.

I do not think that these patients, when they enter the euphoric recall stage, are totally to blame for their non-involvement attitude. The treatment industry is also at fault. Once the patient is detoxed, the basic goal of all types of treatment is to prevent substance relapse. To that end, most treatment follows the timehonored protocols of the past, protocols that were designed for alcoholics and the "disease" of alcoholic addiction.

For those people with a loved one in treatment, you can expect the negative phone calls to start arriving about 15 to 20 days after entry. This is the time when the drugs truly start talking to the addict with the idea that the addict, now detoxed, can control their addiction and/or they seem to think that they can use "one more time." The phone call will claim that the treatment, the food, the accommodations, or something will be very unacceptable to the patient. They will say things like "I can beat this on my own." Trust me, they will be calling.

The hard drug patient, and especially the heroin addicted patient, is a new phenomenon to treatment. In the last five years the treatment facilities began to fill with drug patients rather than alcoholic patients. Therapists have failed to develop new therapy protocols to deal with this new patient. The average patient today in treatment is young, addicted to hard drugs, and struggles to engage in any therapeutic. Hard drugs are much more powerful than alcohol, yet therapy continues to use alcoholic methodology in the centers. I believe the lure of a drug like heroin, and the desire to use again(relapse), is just too strong for contemporary methods of treatment. Statistics support this, as the relapse rate following treatment for hard drug users is over 90 percent.

Therapy is not working.

So when we ask, "How bad is it?" the complete answer must include more than just the failure of law enforcement, the growth of distribution, the lack of rehabilitation in prisons, or the failure of schools to educate. In addition to all of these failures, we have to add the ineffectiveness of our treatment methods.

The end result is that the Opioid Crisis is growing every day. The dealers in our communities are gaining new customers, the prisons release addicts back into the community, our kids do not fear drugs, and our treatment attempts are a disaster. So, the Opioid epidemic is not just *bad*, it's getting worse.

Hard drugs are more powerful than logic, reason, or love. Trying to "talk" a heroin addict into sobriety will not work. They have already been warned about the hazards of drugs from friends, parents, school staff, police, judges, relatives, and others. All of the logic and warnings given to the user from people along the way went unheeded. The addict will not recover until *they truly want to*. The problem here, particularly with the user under thirty, is the fact that they might overdose and die before they recover.

Opioid overdose death usually follows a predictable pattern. In many cases, the addict that overdoses has just been released from a jail term or a rehabilitation facility of some type. They have detoxed and have not used drugs of any kind for a period of thirty or more days. Gaining their freedom, the destructive thoughts begin to surface. Loneliness and boredom begin to surface. The addict begins to believe that they can get high "one more time" and that they can "control their drug use." Thrilled at the idea of getting stoned again, they inject an amount of drug that they used to use, or obtain drugs laced with more powerful Fentanyl. Tragically, the addicts system has adjusted to the "drug free" lifestyle, so the dose taken is too strong. The result is a drug induced coma and, if not treated soon, death.

If you, your family, or your friends have not been affected by the OPIOID crises, you are very fortunate. The epidemic is just about everywhere in America, and growing. I truly wished that treatment would be effective in treating our addicted, but it is not. There will be changes, but not until the huge treatment industry realizes they are failing and start to develop modern applications effective in treating drug addicts. Although our elected representatives are just starting to become aware of the Opioid epidemic, there will have to be a concentrated effort to reverse the threat to our communities. Upcoming statistics and accurately presenting the true depth and extent of the problem will hopefully frighten our government into taking actions that are positive.

Checklist

Below is a checklist you might want to use to determine the possibility of someone developing a hard drug problem. This is not scientific by any means, but will give a general alarm that a problem exists or is developing.

1. Has the individual changed friends recently? Are old friends not coming around, or/and are new friends coming around to visit?
2. Has the individual lost passion for something that was very important in the past, like sports, clubs, or activities?
3. Has the individual been spending more time isolated, or in bed?
4. Has the individual adopted any new habits, such as smoking or vaping? Chewing tobacco?
5. Has the individual lost days at work or school due to being "sick" or tired?
6. Were you involved at any time in calling in excuses for the individual to a workplace or school because they were not going?
7. Has the individual seemed to have a secret or undisclosed lifestyle? Secret texts?
8. Does the individual seem tired or distant most of the time?
9. If the individual is in your home, do they keep strange hours or are they awake at various hours during the night?
10. Has the individual dramatically changed dress or hairstyle recently?

If you have answered "yes" to four or more of these ten questions, I think you might have a problem. If this individual is a child or loved one in your home, the next step is a "search" of their living area and a urine analysis. You have to solidify whether or not a problem exists before you can begin to deal with it, and a test is the finite answer. Remember, the person with the problem will be outraged that you searched their living area and will give all kinds of excuses NOT to take a drug test. The resistance of the individual will also be an indicator of the existence and strength of the problem. The more they protest, the greater the odds that a problem exists.

To help end *American Overdose*, the sooner we identify the problem, the better. If a person begins to display symptoms on the "checklist," they may be at the beginning stages of addiction. The earlier the problem is identified, the easier it is to help them. Addiction is progressive, so all the cravings of increased doses, seeking money, etc., increase with time.

Recreational Marijuana

Pot is a hot topic and has become a political issue in America. I was a teenager in the sixties, and I think I can pretty much say that most people from that era would vote "yes" on a pot referendum. The tide appears to be rolling in favor of the legalization concept, as many states have opened the door on this drug. Of course, whether a state votes yes or not may not make any difference, since here in Arizona we have Colorado to the North, New Mexico to the East, California to the West, and Mexico to the South. All of these areas have recreational pot. We are surrounded, so the availability in Arizona is pretty much a given.

A lot of people ask, "is marijuana a gateway drug?" By this I think they are asking if Marijuana, and the fact that it will be easily obtained, is going to lead to heavier, more dangerous drugs? The answer, is "yes" and also "no."

Evidence exists that suggest that Marijuana or THC (tetrahydrocannabinol) is not addictive. I suppose that is true, not in the sense that opioids and alcohol are. Marijuana is not always physiologically addictive, but one can become psychologically dependent upon it. More than likely, continued daily use of pot and a dependence upon it may simulate an addiction. Most addiction therapists will say that think marijuana is addictive, and for sure, is usually used with other substances. Many hard drugs users will begin a relapse with marijuana, then revert to using their primary drug again. Addicts all tell me that their relapse always begins with marijuana. They say, "hey, it is supposed to be harmless. Then I get high and end right back up on heroin." When recreational Marijuana is available, one can find it in stores in hundreds of different forms. There is coffee with pot, gummy bears, brownies, muffins, cookies, everything. Yes, commerce changes the THC delivery method to make the drug available in many forms. Whether or not legalizing is a benefit to the community is still undetermined, but here are some considerations.

1. THC, the principle drug in marijuana, can cause individuals to be less motivated to accomplish things in life. Daily doses cause individuals to develop an indifference towards accomplishment. Daily heavy users can also experience withdrawals.

2. THC can inhibit reflexes and therefore is intoxicating to an operator of a motor vehicle or heavy machinery.

3. THC can inhibit the brain from making good decisions, so pot can lead an addict back to drinking or drugging with harder substances. Every patient I have treated for hard drug use will always say that smoking pot led to a relapse on cocaine, heroin, or meth.

4. THC can be used while on MAT protocols to get "high," as it's euphoric is not diminished by Suboxone. This means an alcoholic or opioid addict, while taking Naltrexone or Suboxone, can still get high on marijuana. The goal of these medications is to help an addict stay away from drugs, but ease of obtaining pot will promote getting high in manners other than alcohol or opioids. Never forget, getting high is the goal of the addict, the means is whatever is expedient.

5. Legalization of Recreational Marijuana can flood the community with THC items that appear to be a "normal" muffin, brownie or candy, and can be consumed by minors and infants. In some situations evidence suggests that early use of marijuana can create mental problems in later life.

6. Research suggests that use of drugs or alcohol in teens can cause an increasing desire for substances in future years and alters some receptor and brain functions. Some researchers report that adolescent use of substances "opens the door" and creates a propensity towards using substances in the future. Direct evidence of this tendency, however, is still an area of debate and research.

7. While proponents tout that THC is harmless, the fact is that this drug can cause some users to develop panic attacks, chronic anxiety, and long term depression. The data here is somewhat lacking since patients that report to clinics for help with these mental illnesses seldom report the source of their issues as being attributed to initial reactions to marijuana. A certain percentage of users experience "panic attacks"

that are extremely terrifying to the individual. Patients with unknown and preexisting heart problems could feasibly die from a strong panic attack.

8. While proponents of recreational pot continue to claim that the substance is not addictive, it has been my experience that influencing a person to cease the use of Marijuana is difficult. Getting "high" becomes a large part of the users life. We may not call the substance "addictive" in the physiological sense, but we are absolutely correct in deeming it "habit forming."

So, as far as the "gateway drug" question, the answer is solidly "yes" as long as marijuana, beer, tranquilizers, sedatives etc. are all included together. I don't think marijuana can lead directly to heavier drugs, but most people who use it frequently will often sample something more harmful and addictive. The fact that an individual is getting high on any substance may influence them to try other substances that will make them "high" as well. Often, sellers of one drug will have other items for sale.

States that have offered "recreational marijuana" are few, and the long term ramifications are as yet unknown. Colorado is one of these states, and large amounts of data are not yet available to suggest a societal impact one way or another. However, Colorado is experiencing the same growth in drug overdoses as other states, so recreational pot availability has not reduced the use of other, more dangerous drugs. We shall watch Colorado closely in the coming years.

This analyst would question the use of referendums for issues such as recreational pot. Referendums can be dangerous in allowing the public to make decisions by majority vote in an open "yes or no" forum. I am not always confident in the public making the right decisions for themselves. I am not saying that this type of democracy doesn't work, I am saying that some topics could be dangerous if offered to the populace for their opinion. As an example, what if we had a referendum called the "tax referendum?" I think that if you asked America to vote "yes or no" about whether or not we should have any income taxes, most would vote "no." While that might be nice not to have any taxes, it is not very realistic for our society to maintain itself.

Recreational Pot will more than likely alter the substance availability in a "legal" market. Dealers who have been selling potwill turn to other, perhaps more harmful drugs. I don't think a dealer is going to close "shop" just because an income stream has been removed. What this means is that someone will be promoting and distributing heroin, meth, cocaine, and other drugs into communities that were formerly buying marijuana. I suppose we will have to wait and see what happens, but I suspect the outcome may not be positive in the long term. Frankly, adding more fuel to the opioid epidemic cannot be a positive event for the USA.

Marijuana illegally imported into the USA is the number one volume item in the drug smuggling, selling, and distribution world. The reason for this volume dominance is the fact that pot has a lot of users in the US. Dealers will have to find ways to build their businesses with other substance sales in areas where Recreational Marijuana is legal and offered in stores. I suppose we shall have to wait for all the results to unfold, but I have a bad feeling about it. The two biggest damaging substances in America, as far as health issues are concerned, are nicotine and alcohol. These two legal drugs constitute THE major health issues. Now, we are adding another: marijuana. We shall see.

The Addict

Of course, not all of the people in the Psycho/Addiction/Treatment world agree, but there is a building amount of evidence to suggest that addicts seem to all follow uniform behavior patterns. Estimates of American population that are alcohol/drug dependent claim about ten percent of the total population. So there are 30 million or more that are defined as having a substance use disorder (SUD). SUD is the new popular term for a drug problem. I suppose it sounds a little softer.

There are no boundaries to addiction, as it affects the rich, the poor, the brilliant, the less than brilliant, men, women . . . everybody! Like a thick rope that is composed of many small strings, addiction and dependence on substances grows with each using experience. One can easily break a single string of a rope, but twist all the strings together and the rope is untearable. So goes *using*. Each time you drink or use a drug, you are adding a string to your "rope of addiction."

As the strings combine, your addiction becomes more difficult to break. Addiction grows stronger with each substance experience.

If you have a loved one that is an addict, they are not unique and are probably adopting addictive behavior patterns. As addiction grows, so does addictive behavior. Though it may seem that your loved ones would "never do that" the odds are that as addiction grows, so does addictive behavior. Here is the profile of what might be termed the "addictive personality."

1. The basic motivator for addictive behavior is the practice of reaching *outside* of the body to find something that one can put *inside* to make one feel better. This sounds very simple, and it is, but the devastating realization here is that addicts never consider changing themselves inside. They will not work to change how they think, feel, and act. It is always an outside activity, practice, substance, relationship, or

event. Booze, drugs, sex, work, exercise, gambling, food, relationships, money, and shopping are just a few of the items addicts are drawn to to make themselves "feel better." I understand that everyone probably gets a "kick" out of some of these, but the difference is the motive. "Normal" people do not crave or need these outside items to feel good, but addicts do.

2. Addicts never listen to others to try to *understand*, they listen with intent to form a reply. The addict feels compelled to always provide a reply that is somehow better or more intelligent than the other person offers. This will be true in comments, jokes, experiences, opinions or facts. Their intention is to, more or less, be "one up."

3. Addicts are extremely focused on being right. They will go to extremes to prove or argue that they are always correct in views, opinions, statements, facts, etc. This focus is fueled by an extremely low esteem level combined with egomania. They are argumentative about being proven right about something, rather than trying to view issues from another angle. Being proven right makes them feel better.

4. Addicts have relationships not from love, but because they have a distinct purpose. There is no concept of having friends, wives, or lovers just because life is difficult without. The addicts relationships usually have a specific purpose. For instance, a companion may be selected solely by exterior qualities rather than substance, so that being in proximity to them will build one's own image. So men addicts try to have relationships with beautiful women to make them feel better about themselves. The relationships are "dependent" upon something beyond genuine love or affection. Note: divorce is a high possibility in these relationships. Addicts are attracted to a surface appearance. The advanced addict will develop relationships in order to obtain money for drugs.

5. Addicts will always try to control people, places, and things. Their way is always the right way. The addict will always be in charge or be completely quiescent. There is no middle ground. The opposite of "addictive behavior" is "acceptance behavior." Addicts will never be satisfied with something as it is, or accept it. They want to change and mold everything to their visions or motives.

6. Oddly, most addicts remain extremely lonely in life, although they may act just the opposite. In addition, when they are at their most

lonely, they will isolate. Oftentimes, they may just get "under the covers" for a while, or isolate into their own room or bed. The opposite behavior to this would be using a substance and trying to develop a "party time" atmosphere. So for some reason, the addict seems to think that isolation and solitude is somehow a cure for loneliness. Of course, being alone and isolating is *not* the best method for relieving feelings of loneliness, but it is a good way to feel like a continuous *victim*.

7. The addict will always have extreme difficulty is assessing his own situation. He will always feel that he can control his using anytime he wishes. He believes that he is not addicted, and that he has control and power over his life. This attitude will travel with him into treatment and beyond. This continued self-assessment, though completely wrong, will be the biggest hurdle in therapy or treatment. Coincidently, the Twelve Step programs all start with a self-recognition of one's own resistance to the truth. In these programs the patient will be asked to surrender, a most difficult thing to understand or accomplish for the addict.

8. The addict will have a very high boredom level. Underlying the desire to escape is a constant level of boredom, all the time. This bored feeling will manifest itself in increased anxiety levels when the addict is alone, with a group, or at an event. The addict does not have the ability to spend time alone, but also struggles with being in a crowd. The unsettled feeling inside the addict is an urge to "change" their surroundings, although the "change" does not work, since the boredom follows them from one situation to the next. Often, the afflicted will plan a geographic or job change, thinking that a new location or vocation will not include using. Unfortunately, when the addict moves, the addiction moves as well.

9. The addict feels that he is never guilty, that he is never the "problem." I suppose this is part of denial, but surely is an influence to keep using. In statement such as, "The reason I drink is . . ." the blame is focused on a wife, job, whatever. The truth is, that the person drinks or uses drugs because they are an addict.

10. Most addicts are extremely intelligent people. They are crafty and, in many cases, are able to form their lives around their using patterns. Oftentimes, addicts can survive and use for years and years, yet keep

their jobs, pursuits, and families. There is some evidence to suggest that one may "craft" their work and lives around the use of substances. They will pursue a lifestyle in which they are not closely monitored or supervised. Often, they will work "out of their home" or live in a lifestyle that is isolated from judgement.

11. All addicts are liars. This is the most alarming statement to many, but absolutely true. The first person that they are lying to is themselves. They are telling themselves that they are okay and in control of their habit. The second person they lie to is the one that can give them finance, room, or board so they can continue their habit. The stories that an addict will tell in order to get drugs are worthy of some kind of a prize. If you want to hear them, threaten the addict with no more finance, room, meals or any kind of support. You will be amazed.

So there it is, eleven attributes of the addictive personality. When you review this, you may not find all of them apply, but some of the will. Don't forget, the primary goal of the addict in life is to use. Always, they are taking something from the outside in the hopes that it will make them feel better on the inside. The disease of addiction seems to prevent them from looking "inside" to find relief.

The Process of Relapse

Most alcoholics and addicts relapse. It makes little difference how the individual accomplished sobriety. They may have spent a month or more in a residential treatment center, started in Alcoholics Anonymous, or any one of a hundred other treatment pathways. The raw truth is that *most* people in recovery relapse. I believe that it is a part of recovery that we have to accept. Relapse is also the source of most *overdoses*.

We will discuss the various ways for us to adapt to, and accept, the notion of an expected relapse; there are some frightening facts to consider.

First, for any addict using hard drugs such as heroin or black tar heroin, the probability of a lethal overdose in relapse is high. This is because the user will not be physically capable of accepting a very large dose level. Being abstinent for a while, the bodies tolerance declines. Previous dose levels can be too large and strong for the addict to tolerate. In addition, the more recent imports of heroin and black tar heroin are laced with fentanyl, making todays heroins much more powerful. Lethal Overdose is common. In the US, lethal overdoses of heroin have increased three hundred percent in the last few years. In Arizona the last twelve months chart about 1,500 deaths by overdose, and about 6,000 Narcan doses administered. Narcan reverses the opiate's effects, is carried by all first responders here, and is a lifesaver! So, combining both numbers, we had about 7,500 drug overdoses in Arizona in a year, and it is growing! Our little state has about *20 overdoses per day*!

Second, do not be surprised that the relapse may not be a day or two. It may last for months, with all renewed consequences: jail, hospitalization, accidents, etc. Once the addict returns to substance use, he goes on what is called a "run", and the "run" can last a year. Generally, all the old circumstances, health issues, legal issues etc, will return. I think these are

THE PROCESS OF RELAPSE

the most frightening times for the user, when the addiction has truly taken over again and is running wild. This period is also an overdose risk.

Thirdly, the addict will almost instantly return to previous intoxication levels but may require even more of the substance to attain the desired effect. As an example, if an alcoholic was drinking a fifth of Vodka a day, when they relapse they will quickly return to that level of substance intake and more. Most addicts will come to think that they can return to their drug of choice and just use it a little. They will come to believe that they can control it. This idea is totally futile, reckless, and dangerous. Addiction is progressive, and demands more of the substance.

Relapse is not generally an event, but is a process. Normally, it will begin with a cessation or reduction in support group attendance or sobriety community contact. I have never, in my experience, ever met anyone who has stated, "I was going to AA (NA) meetings regularly, and I relapsed!" Every time, when someone relapses, the statement is always "I stopped going to meetings and I relapsed."

The relapse process therefore usually begins with the sobriety support diminishing or ceasing altogether. The voices inside the user's head begins to tell them that they can use or drink "one more time" and the power of denial begins to fire up. Most will believe that they have the power to use their substance of choice responsibly and control it. A most normal thought is usually, "One beer couldn't hurt."

True, for most people, one beer will not hurt. However, for those suffering from the disease of addiction, one beer will absolutely, one hundred percent, lead to bigger things. It will hurt. No one knows why, but that one beer flips some kind of mental switch the addicted person will immediately crave another beer, and then this will lead to a full blown disaster, usually by day's end.

I watch people having a sandwich and a beer for lunch. I have a particular craving for a bratwurst and a beer from time to time. What I will never, never understand, is how someone can order a cold beer in a tall, tall, pilsner glass and only drink a little of it with their meal. They eat, sip, and then stand and leave, abandoning that tall cold glass of beer with most of it remaining. No matter how long I live, I will *never* be able to have a brawt and a beer and leave most of the beer in the glass. *Never.* It is the same for wine in a glass that is left on the table. I promise you that when I was drinking, I would *never* leave any liquid with alcohol in it on our table and walk away. That is because I am an addict. I have a disease. I *know* that if I drink or even sip that first sip, I am "off to the races" with drinking daily.

Okay, so the question remains, "what do we bystanders do when our loved one has a relapse?" I think you have two choices, you can accept that relapse is part of the process, or you can go freaky-teaky and react crazy. Maybe we can look at a sensible reaction to the problem.

Remember, no one can talk an addict out of their substance. Talking and logic is a waste of time. The addict already knows in his soul that he has made a mistake. His addiction-disease thinking has taken over for a while, and the process has to complete its course again.

The addict may use for a few days, a month, or even years. The point of desperation, similar to when the user quit the last time, has to return. The tragedy of relapse is not how bad it is, how long it will last, or if it will have the same ending as before, but whether or not the addict will live through it. Relapse is a most dangerous time in the process of recovery.

Action Plan

Okay, here is the checklist of actions that you want to take when the relapse occurs:

1. Never enable the addict by giving them food, shelter, or money. This will extend his relapse cycle and push the desire for sobriety further away on the calendar.
2. Never allow the addict to "crash" at your home or disrupt your life in any way.
3. Show the addict love at all times, without condemnation. They will generally feel bad enough about the relapse. Tell them you support them fully in recovery, but not at all in relapse.
4. If you are religiously oriented, pray.
5. Make sure the addict knows that you stand ready to support them in another recovery, when the time comes.
6. I want to say this one again. *Never* give them any money. They will have a big story or reason for you to give them finances. They will be very, very convincing. Remember always that addicts are obsessed with obtaining substances, and they need money to purchase. All addicts will lie, cheat, and steal for the substance, so they will be very

creative with reasons for you to give them money. Rest assured, one hundred percent, the user is seeking money for the reason of buying more drugs or alcohol.

The relapse will be a terrifying time for you. There is a danger of injury and/or death during the relapse process. There is very little that you can do about it, and the hardest thing to do, particularly if the addict is your child, is to stand back and watch the process unfold. About all you can do is try to speed the process up by not enabling. One should always clearly communicate the dangers of overdosing and driving while intoxicated. Like I said, pray.

Clinically, the relapser is caught between the power of addiction and the memories of being clean and sober for a period of time. Some clinicians would call relapse a "cry for help." I think it is more of a powerful "lure" of the substance. Addicts are self-medicating, and substances work well as a medication for anxiety, grief, depression, and all negative feelings.

Somewhere during the recovery process, however, the addict has built some psychological resistance to treatment and sober living. The first sign is a discontinuance of meetings. Meeting cessation is a definitive indicator of a relapse in the making. Hey, support meetings are not a big bushel of fun all the time, and sometimes they require a little soul-searching and personal honesty. Honesty sometimes hurts. Substance abusers need support groups to remain sober.

There is always an excuse; the meeting is at the wrong time, it's too far away, the people are not friendly, whatever. To these excuses I always say, "Find another meeting". For example, there are 1600-plus Alcoholics Anonymous meetings every week here in Phoenix. If you do not like one meeting, you can always find another. I have found that any meeting is great if one gives it a chance and keeps going. It will not take long to become comfortable with everyone there.

Every treatment center is focused on one single thing: *preventing relapse*. However, most of them have not come to that realization yet. Most believe that they can change the thinking and behavior of the patient. Obviously, this approach is *not working*.

Maybe this is simplistic, but relapse prevention should be the goal of any program. Usually, the patient in rehab is physically isolated from substances and people who use substances actively. So treatment will detox and provide every patient with the tips, tools, and techniques for avoiding drug or alcohol use. Rol playing, cognitive behavioral therapy, educational meetings, and sobriety living are all part of the protocols in treatment. I hope that these practices influence some to reach long term sobriety, but statistics suggest the hard drug addict is sort of impervious to these protocols. I think the "lure" of hard drugs, like cocaine, heroin, and meth is too strong.

Relapse is, as mentioned before, a "stage" of recovery. The problem with hard drug addicts is not the relapse itself, but whether or not the addict can live through it.

Section 3

Conclusions

Arizona-Specific Statements

THIS SUPPLEMENT ADDRESSES THE Overdose deaths and Opioid Crisis in the State of Arizona. We all see the beauty of our state, the wonderful natural sights and sounds, the fabulous vacation resorts, and the many entertainments available all year long. Lurking beneath the surface, however, is a devastating and growing Opioid Crisis. The Arizona Department of Health Services, by order of Governor Ducey, reports monthly and yearly dat statistics. We all know that most of the drugs coming into our country are from Mexico, and from where I am sitting at this moment, the border is about a hundred miles away. Phoenix is one of the epicenters for receiving and shipping illegal substances to all corners of America. We are sort of a "landing strip" of illegal drug traffic.

Unfortunately, however, it appears that our state is also a ripe and expanding locale for drug use and drug addiction.

Overdose Deaths

Overdose deaths in Arizona, and these would be "reported" deaths, totaled 790 Arizonians in 2016. In May 2018, 1500 deaths have been reported. So, according to reports, overdose deaths have *doubled*. Reported overdose deaths would not include mis-reported deaths *caused* by drugs that may have been reported as a car accident, heart failure, pulmonary issues, drowning, etc. In these cases the patient's death was indirectly caused by substance ingestion, but the coroners actual cause of death may be the physical issues. The actual "reported" numbers may be an understatement.

One thing that is not considered in these overdose death numbers is the number of drug overdose patients that were rescued by administering Naloxone (Narcan) injections. Reported number of Narcan doses administered in the state for the same time period is about 6000. Narcan reverses the effects of opioids, and revives those in overdose. It is a lifesaving medicine, and is carried by almost all first responders here. Police, Fire Departments, and Emergency services all carry the Narcan dose syringes.

There were almost six thousand people found in an overdose that were "saved" by a Narcan injection. If we add the number of deaths with the number "saved" the new total would be about 7,500 per year. This is about *20 overdoses per day in Arizona*!

I wish we could blame so many addictions and overdoses on the Cartels, but they are not the ones to fully blame. May of 2018, there were 316,255 prescriptions written for Opioid pain medications in this state. This is a prescription for one person out of twenty that reside here. If we multiply this prescription number by 21, which is one tablet three times a day (tid) for seven days it equals *6.5 million per month*! This is an incredible volume to leave the drug store and into our homes and communities. Note that all of the 6.5 million opioid tablets are addictive!

Most of the young addicts under thirty started with an opioid pill such as Vicodin, Percocet, or Oxycodone. The wonderful feeling of euphoria lasts a while, then wears off. The kids do not think these drugs are harmful, and start repeating the intake until it becomes physiologically addictive. Next they learn that quartering the pill, adding water, and injecting it is a much stronger and faster way to use the pain killers. Next, the user has problems obtaining the opioid pain killer, and learn that they can buy these drugs and others on the street. They may buy some pain killer pills on the street but then learn that heroin is the "same thing" and works much better. The shift into highly addictive heroin is the beginning of major issues. My heroin addicted patients tell me that if you are a minor, it is easier and cheaper to by heroin in Arizona than a six pack of beer.

I am skeptical enough not to believe that those 6.5 million pills were all used for our "pain." How do people get these drugs? They simply are visiting multiple doctors with the same claim of "pain." Usually the claim is centered around a pain that cannot be measured by an known means. Back pain, shoulder pain, headaches, and leg pain are the most popular. The physician system is under attack from these drug seekers.

The Cartels south of the border have struggled for years trying to keep up with the demand in the USA for marijuana. Pot is the biggest and most profitable product offered by far. Many states now are legalizing what is called "recreational marijuana." To me, this term in itself is a dangerous message to young people, implying that drug use is *okay*. It's *recreational*.

As the states make marijuana available in stores, the Cartels are going to switch the products they offer from marijuana to harder, easier to smuggle, more profitable drugs. I believe that the Cartels began efforts to saturate the suburban and rural markets several years ago. This was a wise business move in anticipation of recreational marijuana. Today, there are millions of hard drug addicts in these outlying areas. Arizona is no exception. Many people in the small desert towns are just stunned by the existence of hard drug addicts in their communities. We have been targeted no less than any other state. We are victims.

BOOK 2

TREATMENT TALK

Treatment Talk

Prologue

THIS BOOK IS FOR the individual considering sending a family member or loved one to treatment for a substance use disorder (SUD). Americans have been caught a little bit by surprise by the Opioid/Drug crisis. Our first reaction, when someone is "discovered" as a drug user, i to send them to "treatment." This book outlines the positive and negatives of treatment and establishes criteria for evaluating whether or not the person would be helped by going.

In addition, *Treatment Talk* offers clear suggestions and guidelines for the person actually going to treatment. I suppose one might call this book some kind of "checklist" to view before physically and financially committing. Treatment is expensive and monthly fees will range from $20,000 to $60,000. Every center will pridefully share how successful they are and how many of their patients are happily in recovery. Unfortunately, few of these claims are true.

Treatment is big business, and some recruiters are on commission for adding patients. The center has a fixed cost for treating fifty patients, so adding another batch of twenty-five patients can turn a struggling operation into a very profitable business. Centers want your business. Arizona just passed a law, making "treatment brokering" illegal. In the past a counselor referring a patient to a specific treatment center might receive a commission. This has been called "patient brokering." Sometimes the "kickback" can be as much as ten or fifteen thousand dollars. As I said, treatment centers are big business, and they want more patients.

Treatment always seems to be the first "cure" that families resort to. Often they are in shock about the discovery of the loved one's addiction and feel that sending the afflicted to a treatment center as soon as possible is the best way to get help. Maybe, and maybe not. In this treatise, levels of addiction will be measured, and protocols other than the expensive treatment protocols will be offered as alternatives.

Families that all of a sudden realize that addiction has come to visit are usually in shock and frightened, with no clear-cut, step-by-step, plan of action. This book hopes to offer the "what to do" in full detail. I hope that in some way, we will help you in these hours of crisis. The goal in *Treatment Talk* is to provide what to know, before you go.

Most patients relapse after treatment, but no one is exactly sure what the rate of relapse is. I would estimate it to be over ninety percent. Alcoholics, I believe, chart better outcomes as the lure of alcohol is much less than the lure of opioids. Heroin is the number one euphoric drug. I believe the attraction of the patient to heroin is just too powerful to overcome using standard treatment methods.

The treatment world, mimicking Alcoholics Anonymous, terms addiction as a "disease." They state that they are looking at addiction in a "disease model." Once we attach the disease term to addictions, such as alcohol, drugs, food, gambling, sex, wine, etc., then we can treat *all of them the same*. This approach is ludicrous, because treating a heroin addict with the same protocols as someone who has a gambling addiction or an eating disorder is ridiculous. Heroin addiction I suppose, can be termed a "disease," but I can assure you that the attraction to heroin is much more powerful than chocolate or slot machines. Maybe they are all diseases, but they are *different kinds of diseases*. A simile would be like classifying the sickness of a strep throat being the same as a broken leg. Yes, they may both be an affliction, but the treatment for each is dramatically, medially different.

I believe that the protocols used in most treatment centers are designed primarily for alcoholics. Drugs, and specifically opioids and heroin addiction, are sort of a surprise to the whole treatment industry, and the assumption from the treatment community is that the standard protocols will work as well for heroin addicts as it has for alcoholics. The problem with this is that the outcomes for treating heroin addicts are miserable. Heroin, and all opioids, are powerful, and they provide euphoria unequaled by any other substance. To treat opioid patients, therefore, the protocols need to be much more powerful than "normal." To date, no new protocols with the strength to battle opioid addictions exist. Simply, I don't think we can counsel or talk someone out of using hard drugs, Heroin, meth, and cocaine seem to be stronger than talk, logic, fear, threats, jail, or other consequences. Even the fear of a drug overdose does not influence the hard drug addict to stop using.

Practitioners love to use the word "addiction" and claim it is a "disease." That is fine, I suppose, but the mental and physiological addiction to heroin cannot be lumped under or treated like the normal "disease" of Addiction. Heroin, and other hard drugs like Methamphetamine, cannot be compared to someone who drinks too much wine. Alcohol can have many different levels of dependency and addiction, while hard drugs often do not. The heroin addict cannot just decide to not use without incomparable cravings and withdrawal consequences.

Statistically, when treating addicted youth, the biggest cure is that they reach the age of thirty. Evidence suggests that most adolescent addicts will stop using at about age thirty. The problem here is that in many cases, with the level or power of today's substances, adolescents may not live that long. While in treatment, the body starts to adjust towards being healthy again, so when the patient leaves treatment and uses, the dose levels are far in excess of what the body is used to. The result is respiratory cessation and death. This overdose event is not uncommon, and overdose deaths are becoming more and more common.

Hard drugs, and heroin in particular, started their national sweep across America about forty-eight months ago. The availability of heroin, and in particular black tar heroin from Mexico, penetrates every city, community, high school, middle school, and neighborhood. Your kids might say that "there are no drugs in our school," but I can assure you that you can buy anything you want in minutes. I know that here in Phoenix, ordering heroin is on -line. One orders, establishing a meeting point, and a car arrives to sell you drugs.

Personally, I do not know where the site is on the Internet, but it does exist. I have had patients relapse using this procurement method to "score" drugs, so I know it is real and functioning.

America is under attack by a very sinister form of commerce. All of the might of the FBI, the DEA, the Coast Guard, Homeland, Presidential proclamations, Border Security, and state and local police, have had little effect in curtailing the amount of drugs brought in and sold in our nation. The problem is bigger and effects more people every month.

Some of the chapters, you will note, are repetitive. So certain chapters contain similar statements to others. The reason for this is that each chapter is designed to be "stand alone" and provide insights into the chapter topic.

While writing the chapter, I could not leave out additional considerations that are relevant to multiple topics.

If you are reading this book, you are probably in a crisis about drug use and abuse. You are not alone. I hope that this treatise provides you with a little sanity and hope.

I understand that there are many treatment professionals, psychiatrists, counselors, and treatment center recruiters that will say that this treatise is all wrong and a waste of time. Maybe so, but the first issue that pervades everything the current "system" is that "no matter what anyone says, drug treatment is *not working*!" When a critic starts to talk, please realize that they are speaking from a failed system, not a working model.

Kent I. Phillips, MSAC, MS, BA, APA
kipphillips46@gmail.com

Section 1

Treatment in General

Introduction to the Reader

This treatise is for the patient, or the supporters of a patient, considering the question of what kind of help to get for an addiction. Every afflicted person has a variety of choices to consider, and each choice is dependent upon the level of addiction, the desire for recovery, the financial position of all involved, and everyone's commitment.

Recovery is a lifelong process; it truly begins when the subject firmly decides to surrender to a program of recovery. There is no "quick cure," but one finite issue of recovery is that we know a lot about addiction and the mental and physical causes. Detox, for instance, is a simple program and generally follows common procedures. I promise you that today's detox protocols allow the patient to easily transition out of the physical aspects of addiction. Detox is unpleasant, but keep in mind that while alcohol withdrawal can be fatal, drug or opioid withdrawal is not, by itself, fatal.

Often detox is conducted under medical supervision from a trained Addiction Physician. Medical detox is highly recommended. Detox is nothing to try to accomplish on one's own. Most addicts are not weak people, but strong people, and they usually feel they can go through detox with no help. Assuredly, independent detox is possible, but a supervised medical detox, with proper medications to ease the transition, is much more pleasant.

One of the detox drugs used is called Suboxone, which is a combination of a drug called Buprenorphine, and a drug called Naltrexone. This drug combination reduces cravings, adds tranquilization, and sort of cleanses the system of substances. This drug combination is highly effective on both alcohol and opioid addictions. The medical detox period can last five to ten days, with a titration off of Suboxone during or following this period. This medically assisted treatment is time honored and very effective, aI think the proper conclusion would be, "folks, don't try this at home," let the professionals do it for you. Just surrender.

This detox phase is pretty common to all recovery protocols. Following this period, the decision will have to be made as to what sort of treatment is most applicable to the patient. I have tried to include a general overview of treatments and the "dos" and "don'ts" of each selection. Like almost everything, there are Cadillac programs and what might be called non-Cadillac programs. They all differ in the type of facility environment and level of attention. I have been involved in recovery for just a few months short of thirty years, and I can absolutely and completely attest to the fact that *all of the recovery modalities will work*. The crucible here to the effectiveness of the treatment is the level of commitment, acceptance, and desires of the patient. The most expensive inpatient treatment facility, overlooking the surf, with daily massages and hot tubs will not help the addict any more than a run-down cubicle room atmosphere in Nebraska in the winter. If the patient is not ready to totally surrender and does not have the will to change, treatment can be more harmful than helpful. The plain truth is that *most people relapse after treatment*. Most relapses are normal, and are part of the recovery process, a hard-hitting consequence that brings the afflicted back into recovery and with new resignation to succeed. The problem with heroin addicts, however, is that the return to one's previous dosage level following treatment can be fatal. Unfortunately, their bodies have adjusted to being drug free and the return to a previous level of drug infusion inhibits the patient's ability to breath.

The key to a relapse is that "a relapse should never be wasted" and that the addict or alcoholic will profit from the experience. In no way am I condoning relapse, as there is always a health risk, no matter what substance is preferred. We must be willing to accept relapse and treat it as part of the process of recovery, not as a failure for all. Frankly, guilt has few positive effects in recovery. Let's stay away from guilt.

One note to parents. No matter what you think, you did not cause your loved one to become addicted to any substance. If your household is filled with arguments, anger, divorce, violence, and totally crazy stuff, it does not mean that your kids will turn to drugs or alcohol. Hey, most houses are filled with all of that crazy stuff, yet only one in ten individuals become addicts/alcoholics. In these cases, the youth are *victims* of availability of alcohol and drugs. Today's youthful addicts will tell you that if one is underage, it is easier and cheaper to obtain heroin than it is a six-pack of beer. Simply, we are under attack by drug cartels and drug distributors. As more states legalize "recreational pot" the dealers will turn to pushing harder drugs for a livelihood. Dealers are not going to just close up shop; they will be handling other more powerful substances.

Black tar heroin is new up and comer, and if you don't believe heroin is in your town, neighborhood and maybe your home, you are mistaken. The Black Tar pushers are very effective!

Today, an adolescent, who will be struggling with all the challenges of growing up with anxiety, depression and self-confidence issues, etc., will find that one little sniff of meth, cocaine, or heroin will magically dissolve any of the scary feelings in just a few seconds. The experience is a powerful discovery of euphoria.

This instant euphoria is the lure and the problem, not your household crazy stuff. Your own guilt about anything will not cure or help anyone.

Whole battalions of soldiers have the same combat experience, yet only a few will suffer from PTSD. In the same way, some people drink or sample all kinds of drugs and seem to not develop addictions; I suppose in the sense that some people tend to get addicted, most people tend to get non-addicted.

Some clinicians spend a lifetime trying to analyze the people that have a propensity to enter addiction. I am not sure why this seems so important, but I guess they feel that it is. It seems more productive to spend time in developing protocols for effective treatment today.

One final and rather depressing comment is that no matter what we are trying to do in America to cure addicts, it's just *not working*. When you hear all this jibber-jabber about Cognitive Behavioral Therapy, psychobabble about Psychotherapy, Altering Thoughts, etc. as part of the treatment center offering, the reality is that nearly everyone relapses after treatment. The alarming fact is that, in reality, treatment is allegedly designed to prevent relapse, and in that endeavor, it fails totally. A good thing, I think, is that key politicians are starting to proclaim an "opioid crisis." So far, it is mostly talk and proclamations rather than actions. We shall see.

The Essence of Recovery

Before we get started with *Treatment Talk*, I think it's important to fully understand something about the individual and recovery. We can send someone to treatment a thousand times; we can beg, threaten, warn, chastise and pray. But always remember: no one will recover unless they have the will to change.

All the logic, talk, begging, counselors, meetings, warnings, jail, hospital visits, treatment centers, divorces, arguments, threats, punishments, money, food, help, rewards, and promises are meaningless unless the addict wants to change and become sober. Of course, no one knows for sure when that will be. Just about everybody relapses following treatment. This relapse, in some cases, can be a final "experiment" with substance use, or it can last for years. Sometimes, the relapse is fatal.

Many people will demonstrate long periods of sobriety between using and drinking binges. We are thankful, at least, for those brief periods of sanity. Remember that addiction is a lifelong disease and is always at play in the mind of the afflicted. If someone is truly willing to change, they have to make a full life commitment to sobriety. Alcoholics Anonymous states "one day at a time" so that the substance abuser does not look beyond the present, and this view has been successful in maintaining sobriety for millions of people. Perhaps it is more realistic to first look at the day and commit to sobriety for this day only.

A key, after accepting the fact that no substance abuser will change without surrendering their *will* to change, suggests a number of rather disappointing facts about the treatment process. Treatment is big business, and there are hundreds of thousands of people working in the "addiction field." There is competition between treatment centers, and there are many "approaches" to recovery. The truth is, whatever they are doing is not working very well. Statistics reflect the raw truth:

- 50 percent of people never show up after scheduling an initial interview.
- 70 to 90 percent of people attending full inpatient treatment centers relapse in the first thirty days after release.
- Death by drug overdoses are up 400 percent nationwide, according to ER data reports. Because of various reporting forms and formats, the real number is much higher.
- Our youth are experimenting with hard drugs such as meth, cocaine, and the most dangerous, heroin (both black tar and China white).
- Drug marketers have switched their emphasis from inner city to suburbia during the last 48 months. The image of driving "downtown" to score is false. Hard drugs are now available everywhere.

The sad conclusion is that our attempts at prevention, control, education or treatment are not working. The treatment industry may boast many victories, but few patients actually recover. The problem is that if the patient is not willing to change, no change will occur. Treatment does go full blast in trying to educate the abuser on the dangers of using, changing thought patterns, and relaxation techniques. Centers claim to be treating co-existing conditions such as anxiety, depression, personality disorders, bipolar, etc. but none of this is working.

Imagine if you owned a business that manufactured a product and 90 percent of what you manufacture was defective and returned after purchase! Your business would close in short order! Yet, we keep sending people to various treatment facilities with continuous failure.

One big question emerges in this discussion—"how do we know if a person is truly sincere about change and sobriety?" The answer is simple—we have no idea! As a society, when a loved one or friend has an addiction problem, we automatically exclaim, "They need to go to treatment!" We should be asking, "Do they want to change?"

Most of the afflicted, when confronted, will always state that they want to be sober and are tired of using. May I suggest that before you send someone to an expensive treatment program, that you try a free one first? In some ways, a free program that requires attendance and commitment will test the abuser's true commitment to being sober. Programs such as Alcoholics Anonymous, Narcotics Anonymous, Sobriety Today, and more are everywhere. As an example, AA has 1,600 meetings every week here in the Phoenix, Area.

Most of these "self-help" programs are free but do require a commitment to change and a will to be substance free in order for them to be effective. The person that is NOT ready to change will go to one of these meetings and report that they will not go back to the meeting because "the people were not very friendly" or "I don't think it will help" or "I can't connect with the people at the meeting" or "I can quit on my own without these meetings!" These comments are really saying, "I am not done using yet." Remember, no one can quit on their own and be happy. Simply, the addicted need help adjusting back into society and understanding why they have become addicted.

Sending someone to treatment can be a positive exercise in that the patient will learn a great deal about drugs, addiction, and alternative ways of living. In years to come, this information and education can be valuable for when the patient actually commits to change and sobriety. Until the patient is ready, nothing said or taught will have much effect.

I am not sure what we are teaching in schools today about drugs, drinking and addictions, but the evidence continues to suggest that most children under the age of 18 have experimented with drugs. There is little use in asking your kids about the level of substance activity in their school they will never tell you the truth. Parents, drugs are everywhere. A recent study completed by the University of Michigan indicates that 60 percent of high school students in the USA have smoked marijuana in the last thirty days

Many people ask about the concept of Marijuana being a "gateway" drug to more serious substances. I don't think there is any evidence to prove that marijuana can cause anyone to move to heavier drugs, but it is definitely on the pathway to harder drug experiences. "Experimenting" with substances as a youth is a danger.

Adolescence is enough of a challenge of anxiety, self-confidence, physical change, family problems, school challenges, etc. One little sniff of cocaine, meth, or heroin dissolves all of these concerns in about 33 seconds. The fact that adolescents are experimenting with pot is enough to alarm me. Experimentation is the beginning of the addiction process. When kids discover how these drugs can make you feel, they are tempted to try stronger substances.

Every hard drug addict I have treated will always say that they started with marijuana. Is pot a gateway drug? Not in the assumption that when one is smoking pot regularly they seek something stronger, but I think this drug opens the door to drug abuse, and abuse opens the door to stronger drugs. Usually a drug dealer that sells pot usually sells stronger, more additive substances. Don't forget these dealer "friends" want you addicted to hard drugs. They are in business to have all of their customers addicted and regular.

Clinically, most counselors can sense if a patient is not engaged in the process. With this type of patient, the therapist is doing what is referred to as "dancing." Dancing means that the treatment professional is working much harder at a patient's recovery than they are. An honest center will confront this type of patient and ask them if they intend to continue with the current attitude. If the attitude is not changed, the patient will be sent home. Treatment centers, in most cases, are interested in income, so a discharge for attitude is pretty rare.

No one can "save" anyone without the patient wanting to change and be willing to work for recovery. Recovery is never granted to a patient who just sits in a chair and listens. The expectation that something in treatment is going to magically reach out and "cure" the patient will never occur. During treatment and after treatment recovery requires a firm, solid commitment to "work" a program. The more one works, the healthier they get. I realize that this may not make a lot of sense to beginners, but all of the support groups, such as Narcotics Anonymous, have an established program.

Sending a Child to Treatment

An immediate reaction of parents who "discover" that their offspring is using drugs is, "We are sending you to treatment so you can get some help!" In most cases, the Affordable Care Act maintains coverage for children under 26 to receive benefits that include inpatient mental health or addiction treatment. The massive increase in drug use in teens, combined with the insurance coverage, creates a relatively new "treatment world." Addiction Treatment Centers have "popped up" in a lot of states, but the most popular geographic locations are Arizona, California, Nevada, and Florida. It has always seemed odd to me that most of these centers are in vacation areas with warm winters. I don't think anyone has a firm statistic on how many different treatment protocols exist, how many people are in treatment at any given time, or any specific statistics on "cure rates". I do know that for the State of Arizona, with six million people, there are 2200 licenses granted to operate treatment environments professionally. That is one license for about every 2500 inhabitants. Some of these treatment centers are big money makers, and offer very nice, hotel-like facilities.

The purpose of this chapter is to present a process prior to sending a friend or loved one to treatment in an inpatient treatment center. There are a number of pros and cons, as well as a number of alternative treatment modalities that I think are important to consider beforehand. Unfortunately, there are no treatments that will be effective on an individual that does not have the will to be sober. I am not sure if I need to repeat, but so we are clear, *there are no treatments that will be effective unless the patient is willing to change and be sober.* Remember, for the addict, sobriety is not a part time thing, it is full time, lifelong The addict does not have the luxury of using for the "weekend" and then stopping. Once they start, the gate is open for a long period of time until they return to you, defeated again.

First, I want to outline the type of help available to just about everyone in the USA. I will outline the service, appraise the service, and qualify the effectiveness of the service. This will be my *opinion* and many may disagree with me. I am trying to be fair as best I can and have no vested interest in one program over another. These are observations

Full Inpatient Treatment Centers

Length of stay can be thirty days, ninety days, or even a whole year. The cost is anywhere from about $20,000 to $60,000 for the first month. These fees seem very high, but also generally include a lot of medical testing, individual diagnostics, and assessments. Subsequent months are generally less costly. Good health and sobriety go hand in hand, and many addicts need a little repair physically as well as mentally. Most centers have a number of medical professionals and doctors on staff to diagnose and serve the patient.

The inpatient center is a 24/7 treatment protocol, with the patient staying in a dorm or a house with full day supervision, meals, bedding, hygiene, and activities. Eyes are pretty much never taken off of the patient during their stay. Some offer extra activities, such as boating, camping, hiking, horseback riding, etc. The big variable in this setting is the cost, with the most expensive ones being similar to a fancy resort, and the less expensive being quite a bit less than a fancy resort. I think you get the picture.

Do the expensive, fancy resort type facilities offer better curative services than the cheaper ones? No, I don't think so: it all depends on the patient. Frankly, no matter how nice the facility is, your loved one will probably call home with some complaints. These calls and complaints do not realistically evaluate the center at all. They are spawned by the patient's desire to leave and get high. If the patient is committed, the surroundings will not matter at all. They will be totally engaged in the process of recovery. I think all of the employees of these centers are about the same, in that they are totally committed to the success of the patient and rejoice when a patient can return years later with a drug or alcohol free life. The attitude of help and understanding permeates every therapist and worker. Few if any are paid a lot, and in most cases underpaid. You will like and admire the staff in most cases. Don't listen to any complaints from your loved one it is the drugs talking, and in some cases they are talking very loudly. Remember that after ten days or so in rehab, the patient has detoxed fully. At this point the addict starts to fantasize about using again and getting high. This is the time frame when he/she will call home with the complaints and disappointments, as well as statements such as: "I can lick this on my own! I am not learning anything here!" This is what I mean when I say that the drugs are talking.

A day in the life at inpatient is sort of like this, though all are different. Most resemble a "Boot camp" of sorts with daily regimented activities:

Morning

The day will probably start early, about six or so. Patients will have a blood pressure check, any medications they are supposed to receive and a general "check in" with a technician.

Breakfast

The rest of the morning will probably consist of dorm or house sized groups, one -onone individual therapy, an educational lecture, and a small group composed of people with the same issues of addiction.

Lunch

The afternoon will be some type of exercise, maybe an activity. Yoga, meditation, biofeedback, dietetic consultation with a nutritionist or a psychiatrist not uncommon. Plus there may be a lecture followed by a process group, discussing the lecture. Sometimes, there are special "add-ons", such as horseback riding, rafting, boating, camping, conclaves, etc. offered. These "extras" can be charged to the patient at the end of treatment, and can be quite a financial blow to the payer. Insurance will never cover these extra services. Beware.

Dinner

In the evening, patients will be transported to an Alcoholics Anonymous or Narcotics Anonymous meeting, or there may be one held on campus or in the house. Twelve step groups are usually an integral part of a recovery center. Statistically, if a patient does not attend some type of aftercare sessions or group, their chance of long-term sobriety is zero.

Weekend

The weekend may be filled with an outside activity, visitors from home, camping with your house or roommates, boating, etc. These activities depend upon where your center is located and may create extra charges for you.

Inpatient Treatment Center Pros and Cons

Pros

The inpatient center is a "crash course" in recovery. An excellent experience for the first-time patient to be exposed to the feelings of sobriety, the nature of being in sobriety, and experiencing support groups. For someone that has never attempted sobriety before, it is an excellent educational, therapeutic, and healthy experience. I suppose my theory is that an addict should be treated by considering cost first and effectiveness second. If the addict truly has a real intent of becoming sober for life, then a good test is to start at the bottom, with free support group attendance, then move up to Intensive Outpatient treatment.

There is also a certain level of new friendships and camaraderie developed during the stay. The friends made here often stay in touch for the rest of their lives.

For severe drug addicts or alcoholics, this is the first time they have been medically and safely detoxed during their addiction cycle. This period, however brief, impacts the patient in a way that demonstrates the feelings and attitudes that they had before they started using. In addition, patients can learn valuable lessons in relaxation therapy, yoga, and meditation, as well as cognitive alteration to do other things in place of drugs or alcohol. The time is a "peek" into sober life, with few outside abstractions.

Another pro is that for the patient cannot be influenced by a "bad crowd" of friends that are still using. The Inpatient treatment might be absolutely necessary to create a physical and mental break from this environment. Other treatment methods do not provide any type of health isolation from what might be called a toxic atmosphere. Someone should make this decision close to the patient, and not the patient.

Inpatient treatment also provides very close medical and psychiatric care. Detox is closely monitored and often medicated, making the first portion of treatment less unpleasant.

Another positive here, and I mention this delicately, is that inpatient offers a decent "break" for the rest of the family in situations where the addict has been incorrigible. I know we all love our family members, but sometimes a family might truly need a little "break" from the crazy stuff.

Cons

Of course, one of the cons is the statistical inference of the number of patients who relapse following treatment. I am not going to share this with you, because the number is large and very frightening. If one looks at the relapse curve only, the evidence would strongly indicate that inpatient treatment centers are a waste of money and time. This relapse probability is true, *unless* the patient is committed to being healthy again and is compliant in attending support groups immediately following treatment. If the loved one comes home, and immediately says., "Oh no, No AA for me," then you know you are in trouble, because the addiction will return in force. Guaranteed.

Of course, the other negative is the immense cost of these inpatient modalities. To have all of the individual group service, room and board, medical attention, twenty-four seven monitoring, and nice facility arrangements costs a lot. So again, we come back to the big question about the patient's seriousness towards recovery.

Intensive Outpatient Treatment

In most states, the level and modality of care is defined by state statutes, so when the term "Intensive Outpatient" is used, the treatment follows some strict guidelines. Most of these treatment centers provide individual therapy and group therapy on a regular basis each week, but the patients are not in a dorm or house as far as living is concerned. This type of treatment is ideal for those that want to keep on working, schooling, or living a normal life while still experiencing some powerful therapy.

Pros

IOP (Intensive Outpatient Therapy) provides a confidential and therapeutic treatment protocol without sending someone to a full-service treatment center. Detox in this type of protocol is accomplished *before* admission, or can be ideal for the abuser who may not need a full medical detox. Remember, alcohol detox can be *fatal* if not medically supervised; drug detox is more severe in some ways, but is *not* fatal. Every case is different and requires professional assessment.

Many people remain in IOP for long periods of time; it is inexpensive and covered by most health insurance companies. The center will be responsible for detailed progress reports to your insurance companies and maintaining a high standard of care. IOP provides a very flexible treatment modality that can adapt to the patient's lifestyle.

Cons

Of course, the biggest con is that the patient can simply stop coming. I will guarantee that every addict or alcoholic will experience a special feeling soon after detox. This general feeling or thought is, "you know what, I can control this! I am okay now." I wish this thinking were accurate, but it is not. No: if you are an addict or an alcoholic, *you can't have just one*. One will never work. Many addicts returning to treatment following a devastating relapse will most often say "it all started with a beer." Every time the process of getting high happens with a beer or smoking pot or whatever. This re-adventure leads to another, and another, and then one is right back to their original habit levels of destruction.

When this special feeling surfaces in the patient, this is the exact time that they should *not* cease treatment. You will clearly witness these moments in your loved ones. It is not the patient talking or thinking, it is the substance talking or thinking. It is always there, always.

There are many people that can benefit from IOP and lots of patients who are in the full treatment center therapy will continue on with IOP for long periods after release from inpatient. IOP provides an ongoing attachment for recovery and professional therapists.

Medically Assisted Outpatient Therapy

This protocol is rapidly growing all over the United States for alcoholic and opioid addicts. This treatment is the same structure as outpatient or some modification of the protocols with one single but very important difference. While the patient is still undergoing some type of counseling, they are also being administered an antagonist drug such as Suboxone. This drug prohibits the dopamine receptors in the brain from generating the feelings of getting high on alcohol or opioids. This means simply that the patient cannot really relapse, because if they are properly dosed, they cannot feel a "high."

An important issue in this protocol is the absolute necessity for professional addiction counseling! There is a significant adjustment for the patient to return to a sober life. Always remember that most addicts are suffering from other mental issues in addition to addiction. Many patients began their journey in addiction through self-medicating depression, anxiety, or other mental issues. These can be addressed once the patient has detoxed and is physically free from the influence of the drug. The counselor will be prepared for any emergence of comorbidity, and can refer the patient to other specialists.

Pros

If the patient continually follows dosing directions, they are pretty much immune to the effect of alcohol or opioids. In other words, an alcoholic can go to a party, drink a beer or two, and the alcohol will have NO effect. The same antagonist prevents getting high from any opioid, including heroin, fentanyl, morphine, oxycodone, vicodin, percocet, etc.

Medically Assisted Therapy (MAT) is ideal for the person that truly wants to be sober, continue their lives as a father or mother, work, schooling, sports, etc. and can remain fully confidential. The medications have to be physician administered and monitored, but the patient is totally free to live their life unaffected by a relapse or slip. They can have daily medications, injections that last a month, or new implants that may last up to six months.

In many cases, this protocol might be considered prior to admission to a treatment center inpatient program, as it assesses the patient's true desire to gain abstinence. On this protocol, the primary reason anyone would discontinue the medication is to regain a "high" feeling again. So this protocol quickly determines if the alcoholic or opioid addict is truly wanting to leave the life of addiction or not.

The advantage of this protocol over others is the cost, which would be about one third of that for a Full Year of treatment compared to ONE Month of inpatient treatment.

Cons

Maybe the biggest negative to this protocol is the fact that the patient is not removed mentally or physically from their current life and current life stressors. This is why ongoing therapy is necessary. Although the addictive substance may be removed, psychodynamic therapy is needed to develop coping skills. The patient is going to have to establish a new lifestyle and habits, as they control his/her destiny.

Another negative is that the patient can time their capability of getting high. On the oral daily medication, the patient could miss a dose on Saturday morning and feasibly get high or drunk on Saturday night, although they may return to daily dosing on Sunday morning. Addicts are probably the sneakiest people on the planet when it comes to using, so certain creative events are to be expected. The counterpoint that is positive is an injection of a longer acting medicine, such as Vivitrol.

Another negative about the Medically Assisted programs is that the patient can still get loaded on drugs that are not opioids or alcohol. To date, the medicines available are effective on the consumption of alcohol or an opioid. These two cover a lot of patients, since they are the most common drugs; however they do not minimize any effect of marijuana, ecstasy, cocaine, tranquilizers, and others. The list of these drugs is very long. Addicts, therefore, CAN get high on other substances. Patients are required to take random urine analyses and can be expelled from the program.

One positive consideration is of all the days, weeks, or months the patient was without substances, so the MAT is still a major improvement. If an addict is spared drug use for any length of time, it is still a victory of sorts.

Medically Assisted Therapy is not really anything new, nor is the drug Naltrexone/Buprenorphine. Of course, the Addiction Treatment Industry is mostly negative about it because this protocol REPLACES the treatment center and provides an inexpensive alternative to inpatient. There is a massive industry built around treatment centers that is threatened by MAT.

An important weakness in the MAT protocol is the fact that patients can use Non-Opioid/Alcohol drugs with no consequence. Marijuana, Cocaine, Meth, etc. can be used at will since the patient is not monitored. The danger here is the fact that these drugs will usually lead the patient back to their drug of choice. As mentioned before, the act of getting high is a danger in itself, as getting high by any means can often influence the addict to return to their drug of choice.

Support Groups

Some find support groups to be the best avenue for recovery and sobriety. Support groups are of many varieties, including religious groups, Alcoholics Anonymous, Narcotics Anonymous, Heroin Anonymous, etc. These groups operate pretty much everywhere in the USA and many places around the earth. They can be found on Google for any city. Many people eventually end up in these support groups following other treatment experiences, due to the fact that treatment alone is not going to provide an ongoing freedom from substances, and all addicts or alcoholics need a continuing support group to maintain sobriety. In almost all cases, these support groups are free and supported primarily by small donations from each attendee. This small donation is almost always one dollar, or maybe two. The donations are always voluntary.

Meeting places can offer daily groups, weekly groups, and are sometimes held in churches or in specific group facilities. The facilities often provide group meetings around the clock or close to it.

Pros

The biggest pro about support groups is probably the fact that they are free. The second biggest pro is that these sessions, usually lasting about one hour each, are pretty much everywhere. Most groups follow the same twelve-step concept that is in the Alcoholics Anonymous presentation. I have found that most of the groups that have Anonymous in their name, like Narcotics Anonymous, etc. are very close in practice to a basic AA meeting, so I am not sure if one is better or more applicable than the other. The difference is the substance of addiction, and generally the age groups in attendance.

Another pro or positive to these support groups is that adherents and attendees tend to adapt to a new serenity, lifestyle, and code of behavior influenced by the group's traditions. My personal experience is that I have been in AA for thirty years, and I still attend a meeting weekly.

It seems that support groups provide a special "community" that offer a feeling of belonging, and being around people with similar problems is positive and helpful.

Cons

One of the negatives of these groups is that there is no control over the addict/alcoholic maintaining attendance. While sometimes attendees are "court ordered," almost everyone is there on a voluntary basis. Sometimes youthful drug addicts attend an Alcoholics Anonymous meeting filled with older former alcoholics and find it difficult to engage in the process. To those the best thing is to *find another meeting*. The number of meetings available suggests that everyone can find someplace they will feel comfortable. As an example, in Phoenix, Arizona, there are 1600 plus AA meetings per week.

Some people might say, since they may have been required to attend meetings while in treatment, that "AA just won't work for me!" This comment is totally understandable if the patient is expecting that some magical cure will be offered just by walking into these rooms. There is no magic in the AA program, just some suggestions that an individual can follow to obtain sobriety and serenity. It seems obvious to me that if someone thinks that these voluntary programs won't work for him or her that they have not taken the program very seriously. Free programs require work and commitment. Most groups have a twelve-step process that is delivered as a suggested method of recovery. Usually this process requires working the "steps" and can be emotional, challenging, and self-revealing. Nothing will "save" the addict. In any treatment, the patients have to work to "save" themselves.

Addiction Therapist

This program is sort of like an IOP program but usually is only one-on-one sessions with a specific counselor. These sessions are designed to help individuals live without the use of substances and thrive in sobriety. The duration of these personal therapeutic treatments can be for years and years if necessary. This protocol is like MAT, but usually without the aid of medications and provide much more individual therapy sessions and attention. They do not require an MD for this process and can be conducted by an "addiction coach," as well as a licensed counselor. The key here is how much the counselor or coach interacts with the patient.

Pros

The major advantage of this approach is the personal development and revision of a customized singular treatment plan, designed around the patient. As substances are removed from the individual, co-existing mental issues may surface and be recognized and treated in individual sessions. The therapist is not following any specific format and may refer the patient to other specialists in mental health and can aid the patient in many ways during the path to sobriety.

Another advantage to individual therapy is the fact that it is confidential and private and does not require the patient to "disappear" for a time in a treatment center. Also, the progress of the patient can be documented, analyzed, and singular, so that the protocol can be altered to fit the individual continually. There is no true "standard program" that the patient needs to adapt to; the program is designed around the patient.

In general, an observer will notice a significant "change" in the patient after a few sessions of the therapy is effective. This "change" could be facial expression, level of physical relaxation, or general demeanor.

Cons

The most common complaints about the private therapy protocol is the time and the expense. Progress can be very slow and may require more assessment, diagnosis, and treatment, all requiring payment for services. Therapy can continue for years, depending upon the case. A successful therapist/patient relationship is absolutely necessary in this protocol. A mutual level of trust, honesty, surrender, and commitment is required in the relationship.

Private therapy can be very intense and mentally taxing. Remember here that the therapist is targeting ONE person and has in-depth knowledge of this specific patient. Sessions can be very mentally taxing and could be almost "painful" from a discovery and dealing with this discovery in an honest manner. Frankly, individual addiction therapy can be a real challenge for the patient and require and ongoing mutual understanding and respect between therapist and patient.

In general, the private therapy method is an excellent way to obtain a specialized and direct treatment plan, implemented over a fairly long time period. The results can be very positive, but the patient must maintain a high level of trust towards the therapist, and often trust is not easy for the addict in recovery.

Choosing the Best Course of Therapeutic Action

My opinion will always hinge on the level of commitment the patient has for recovery. I automatically assume that in almost all cases, what the afflicted is *saying* is not true.

Alcoholic/Addicts will say just about anything to alter their current lifestyle. Often the exclamations that the loved one is ready to change are usually predicated not on an innate desire to obtain sobriety, but out of fear for the situation developed through abusing a substance. Jail time, prosecution, fines, etc., are just a few of the reasons a loved one is asking for help.

America's initial reaction to the discovery of addiction is to send them off to a treatment center! In most cases, an insurance company is paying a lot of the bill for services. While this reaction solves several immediate problems, such as removing the addict from your world, this practice has yielded few results. So my opinion is based upon the fact that we have no way of knowing or measuring anyone's true, sincere commitment to sobriety.

With this unknown in mind, it seems sensible to me to start at the bottom and work one's way up in terms of expense. By that I mean start with free support groups, then an individual therapist, then Medically Assisted Therapy, then a short term in a full blast treatment center.

During the early phases of treatment, expect relapse (in a separate chapter), but pay even closer attention to how quickly the afflicted one returns from the relapse and returns to treatment. The shorter the relapse time, the more hopeful we become. Realize that addiction treatment is a process, not a single event. I guarantee that for all addicts, regardless of substance preferred, Recovery is a lifelong pursuit and not something that can be "cured" by a month or two of inpatient treatment.

I want to reemphasize the point that treatment is life-long. This means that more than likely the addict will have to attend support meetings for the rest of their lives. They may not like it, but if they are determined to the sober life, meetings will be a part of it. This may seem like a very long and hard task, but all the people I know that become familiar with the Twelve Step Program, from Doctors to Dumpster Divers, all have regular meetings as a foundation of their sobriety.

Who Should Go?

IF YOU ARE HEADED for treatment, there are a number of things to consider before you financially commit.

The first and foremost question is whether or not the patient is truly committed to recovery and is ready to learn how to live a drug or alcohol-free life. Please realize that this is the most difficult, if not impossible, thing to determine in advance. By the time one reaches the point in their lives that inpatient treatment seems to be the only option, they will probably say that they would do anything to be free from their affliction. Anything.

However, once someone is in treatment and completed detox, the power of addiction starts to surface again. Addiction has its own voice, and the voice is telling the patient that "you can use or drink one more time" and that "it's okay now, you can control it." This will occur in every patient's experience. This self-destructive thinking usually hits about seven to ten days at the end of the detox cycle. The patient will then start calling home. They will claim that something is wrong with the center, the counselors, or 12 step meetings These calls mean that they are ready to leave treatment and relapse. It is a dangerous time.

Most centers utilize a "twelve step program," and patients will probably attend local meetings. In many cases, this will be a patient's first experience to any kind of "group help." Unfortunately, these groups, such as Alcoholics Anonymous and Narcotics Anonymous, are an addict's lifelong requirement, because they are the only "free" aftercare aid for long-term sobriety. If the patient is complaining about it now, they probably are not serious about recovery anymore.

Following treatment, the success rate of maintaining sobriety without attending these support groups regularly is just about zero. If a patient is saying that they will "never go to these group meetings," they probably aren't truly committed to recovery. Before you send the check off to a thirty-day center, you might find out how they feel about going to meetings now and in the future. If one is already opposed to attendance, their chances of long term recovery are very small. Spending money for treatment will be a bad investment. The entire focus in treatment, when the patient is secluded and free from drugs and alcohol, is to teach them how *not* to relapse.

To that end, the afflicted will learn how to deal with anxiety, stress, forgiveness, relaxation, negative or harmful thought processes, diet, and exercise. Without follow up work and attending support meetings, most of these learned assets diminish and drift from memory. Addiction, with all of its power, returns in full force and the victim just doesn't have a chance. Relapse is more prevalent in Opioid addiction, as the power or attraction to these drugs is the most overwhelming. I have never heard a person in Alcoholics Anonymous glorify drinking. Never have I heard anyone say, "I used to drink two fifths of Vodka a day, and it was great!" Hard drug patients, however, particularly heroin addicts, glamorize getting "high" to the point that there is some kind of euphoric recall in even discussing the stoned memories of getting "high." From a counselor's standpoint, this euphoric recall capability is very disturbing and totally interrupts any type of recover protocol or progress.

One of the problems associated with the four-week inpatient treatment program is that the first week, the patient is detoxing and confused. This initial week is not very effective. The second week is spent more or less getting acclimated to the daily activities; the third week is truly spent in recovery, and the fourth week the patient is mostly thinking about going home. So the reality is the addict only gets *one week* of help. I realize that each person is different, but this is a general comment and observation. The problem is that most people in treatment don't truly pay much attention to what is going on.

An average day is getting up early, getting appropriate medications, attending lecture, small group sessions, yoga, lecture, AA or NA meetings, and fellowship. These experiences become a blur and seem repetitive. The reason for this is that the *addict* is by nature, *defiant*. Concepts are basically "hammered" into the patients mind so that they might benefit from the instruction in the future when they are not in a treatment facility. This is the hope of treatment. If a person getting ready for treatment is reading this treatise, then I say to you that if you go, really pay attention.

A Typical Day in a Treatment Center

You are going to have busy days in treatment. Most centers have you wake up quite early, about 6 a.m. or so. You take a shower and get dressed, make your bed and clean your room, then go to *medical*. Your blood pressure is taken and any prescribed medications are given at this time.

Next you have breakfast, and then start your treatment day. A sample day might look like this:

- Seven AM: Dorm discussion or house discussion and process group
- Eight AM.: Individual counseling with a therapist one on one
- Ten AM: Small group of same sex, with similar addictions with counselor
- NOON: Lunch till One thirty
- One thirty: Yoga or Relaxation therapy
- Three: Gym and exercise
- Five: End of day processing with other dorm members
- Six: Dinner
- Seven thirty: Twelve-step attendance off of campus
- Nine: Return to housing, free time
- Ten: Lights out.

This is a normal day in treatment. In some ways, the day is tiring when one is opening some of their inner self to others. Exercise is important, as well as nutrition.

Pay Attention Every Day

Within a week to ten days in treatment, one will begin to feel pretty good mentally and physically; most centers feed the residents well, exercise them, and teach them coping skills so they become pretty confident and positive. This schedule of feeling good is exactly when the addict side of our brain starts to give us several little destructive messages. Specifically these are:

- "Hey you feel great, I think you can use one more time if you wish."

- "You can control this, and just drink or use when you want to, you've got this."
- "You are starting your life over, you can drink or drug if you want to."

And I guarantee that everyone in treatment gets the same destructive messages that seem so real; they are difficult to ignore. Hard drug addicts, as opposed to alcoholics, are influenced by these thoughts to the maximum. Most of the time, they are overwhelmed.

Treatment on an inpatient basis is relatively short term compared to a lifetime. The protocols are intensive and repeated day after day. The hope is that some of the learning will "sink into the addict's brain" and modify behavior, and a huge benefit to a center is that the patient is isolated from the outside world. The problem is, however, that the outside world is going on just as it was day after day, and at the end of treatment, the patient is ejected right back into his/her world. While the patient may have changed his thinking patterns, the outside world is exactly the same as when he left it. The same people, the same stress, the same sights and sounds, and the same temptations await. The hope is that the patient will learn to adapt to his surroundings *without* using drugs or alcohol.

Since the world hasn't changed, the recommendation will always be, when the patient has completed inpatient treatment, to continue on with Intensive Outpatient Treatment (IOP) and/or support group meetings.

Inpatient Treatment? Yes or No?

Note that no matter what kind of treatment method is chosen, the patient always ends up back in support groups. Remember I mentioned that it was difficult to determine if a loved one is truly committed to sobriety? Well here is a simple recommended test that might be something to try as a first step in recovery. Since the addict is saying that they are committed to being sober, send them to some support group meetings and see how they respond to that! Alcoholics Anonymous is a very old and time-tested group for recovery. Narcotics Anonymous is a sister group structure working with the same principles as AA.

Some people can start in AA and never drink again. Some people can go to a meeting of NA or AA and state emphatically, "That's not for me!!" So that we are all together, I live in Phoenix, Arizona, and there are over 1600 AA meetings every week in this city. If someone goes to a meeting and doesn't like it, I quickly suggest that they pick another one. Sometimes the addict does not feel comfortable in one meeting environment, but there are so many, at least ONE will prove positive.

What I am saying here is that sending the patient to these support groups BEFORE spending a big batch of money on inpatient treatment might be a method of measuring the commitment to sobriety level in the individual. Another method of determining commitment, and also of getting rapid results is Medically Assisted Treatment.

Medically Assisted Treatment

While this concept is not new, it has always been an issue of controversy in the treatment community. Medically Assisted Treatment, (MAT) is a simple process: the patient is administered a drug by mouth, by injection, or as an implant under the skin, depending upon the effective time of treatment is desired. Usually this drug will be Suboxone, a combination of Buprenorphine and Naltrexone, or Naltrexone by itself. These drugs block the receptors in the brain, and amazingly enough, prohibit the patient from any feelings of "high" when they use alcohol or an opioid. I realize that this sounds amazing, but it is absolutely true. This protocol will include therapy on a consistent basis with a qualified addiction counselor, and, as long as the patient remains taking the drug and attending therapy, the results are pretty much one hundred percent!

Some of the advantages to the MAT protocol are:

1. The patient can continue with work, school, sports, or any activities without having to be secluded in a treatment center.
2. If the patient relapses on opioids or alcohol, they will not experience a "high" or a "buzz" at all. Relapse, therefore, does not exist in the traditional sense.
3. The drugs tend to reduce cravings in the individual.
4. This protocol allows the addict to develop a drug-free new lifestyle, and more or less forces the patient to change.
5. There is no community stigma of being in recovery. The patient does not have to admit they have a problem to anyone and disappear for a month or so in a center.

6. This treatment is totally confidential between the therapist and the patient.
7. MAT is administered by a physician.

So, prior to making a significant financial or time commitment, there are several options to consider prior to sending someone to inpatient. The counter argument in favor of a treatment center protocol is that the center removes the addict from their surroundings. If the situation is such that the immediate surroundings of the patient are destructive and toxic, then the isolation and separation of a center may be the best avenue for recovery. Each person is unique and special in circumstances.

Always make your treatment decisions with the help of an Addiction Coach or an Addiction Counselor. There are more detailed descriptions of types of treatment in the previous chapter. I think the answer to the general question of "who should go to treatment?" is dependent on a few conditions. Specifically, these are:

1. Patience: if you can't take it anymore, inpatient is the ideal place to send your loved one. This might sound heartless, but if you need a break, this works.
2. Cost: if you can't afford inpatient, consider Medically Assisted Therapy with the patient living in a sober home.
3. Addiction Level: if the patient is incorrigible, they need to go to detox immediately. Other psychological issues may not be determined if the patient is on drugs. Detox will enable a professional to diagnose and assess.
4. Domestic Conflicts: if domestic conflicts exist between the addict and others who are in outpatient protocols, it might be best to send them to inpatient treatment.
5. Support Groups: these are important and critical for long-term success. These groups are for *everyone* in the family. The addict or alcoholic will need to go to these meetings for the rest of their lives, however Al-Anon is an excellent meeting for the people that have to live with the afflicted. Al-Anon will teach one how to cope with addicted loved ones and aid you in what to do to help the addict recover. Addiction is a family problem, and no one is immune. Get Help.

Rehab and Fantasies

When someone is admitted to an in-patient treatment center, they are robbed of everything that might identify them, or act as an identity item. In the normal day, we have all kinds of possessions and accomplishments that enhance our personalities: houses, cars, toys, clothing, jobs, awards, community reputation, schooling, titles, and other physical possessions. In treatment, all you have is yourself and a few clothing items.

Most people's identities are dependent upon their surroundings and possessions. Clothing, Car, are a house all are a statement of who a person is and where they stand in the local socio/economic setting. When one arrives in treatment, all of these things are removed. In fact, most treatment centers will search your baggage and confiscate any medications, phones, weapons, lotions, mouthwash, tonics, and anything else that is not in accordance with the treatment facilities rules. I suppose we might say that everyone is on an equal footing.

For some, this loss of rank and prestige is difficult to live with, so they will invent fantasies. Some will claim they used to work for the CIA, the FBI, served on the board of the treatment institution, are wealthy and have multiple houses, etc. There is no limit to how big the stories can be, all designed to make the person stand out from the crowd and gain prestige. The safest assumption is not to believe anything; whether a story is true or false, it truly does not matter, because you should be working on your own recovery every day.

When I was in treatment, there would be some that would talk openly about how successful and accomplished they were in the outside world. As a check against this, we would always say: "and no matter what else you do, right now you are in an *Alcohol and Drug Treatment Center*. This would always help everyone to refocus in a more realistic manner, because everyone in the center was the *same*. We all had a problem with drugs or alcohol or both.

No matter how grand one's life was on the outside, right *now* they are fighting for their lives in recovery and treatment. Addiction is a "leveling" influence that cannot be denied. No matter what someone was on the outside, they are just another patient here in treatment.

When you enter treatment, I think it is a good learning exercise to observe how powerful egos surface is some individuals. *Ego* is an addict's enemy, and the first entity that should be abandoned for sober health.

They are a lesson in how powerful addiction is and what it makes people do. In this case, people are creating something from the outside, to make them feel better on the inside, rather than focusing on the inside, where the problem exists. Ego takes control of some, and they want to try to project something they are not.

Often the fantasy can be from someone with whom you develop a romantic relationship. Imagine that when treatment is over you discover that the story you were told was completely false. You have fallen in love with a fantasy that does not exist in the outside world. These kinds of relationships crumble very quickly after treatment ends. Romance in treatment is quite common, because again, we are sort of "cut off" from the outside world. As one expert says, "the odds are good you will fall in love in treatment, just always remember, the goods are odd!"

Addicts are usually thrill seekers, taking something from the outside to make them feel better on the inside, and just checking in to a center will not alter one's behavior. Removing substances from the person will probably not alter their addictive behaviors either.

The reason this chapter is included here is that it is important to observe the others in treatment and how fantasies continue to flourish. Watching this behavior and understanding that addictive behavior spawns is important to your recovery, in that behavior demonstrates the power of addiction. Fantasies are not damaging to one, as long as the person realizes they are just there as imagination. When fantasies are harmful is when they are used almost like a drug to make someone feel better. I often imagine I am a downhill ski racer, but I am actually afraid of heights, and I hate cold. Go figure.

Addicts use many actions to make themselves feel better: fantasies, food, exercise, gambling, power, and sexual conquest, to name a few. While I suppose that all of these things are sort of okay in normal quantities, the addict uses them as an ointment. They are something to apply to alter one's feelings. Addicts alter their moods by extremes. Sometimes addicts will react with an "over the top" approach, such as in Alcoholics Anonymous when the person attending will get super involved and almost fanatical in his support. While this is an addictive behavior that can yield positive results, remember that fanaticism is *replacing* something else, like drugs and/or alcohol. Zealousness in AA is good, but be careful that it does not turn into a negative. Remember that gamblers get the same thrill from winning as they do losing. They are seeking a thrill, good or bad.

Religiosity in treatment is never a bad thing, unless it is carried to an extreme. Of course, there are many "reformed" addicts who claim sobriety was delivered to them by a deity. However one gets to the point of recovery is fine, but what happens if the person stops believing? Loss of religiosity can be a cause of relapse, since one's recovery is not fully dependent upon the individual's commitment and surrender. Personally, I applaud people who have faith, as I think strong faith in a deity helps us with serenity and order. I wish that I possessed this kind of faith.

The key point in recovery and treatment is to not allow diversions to enter your program. Recovery can happen without some great miracle occurring, so I wouldn't wait around for the skies to open. They probably won't. In treatment, pay close attention to the program and *your recovery*. Stay away from diversions in treatment, and there will be many. Do not listen to those condemning some part of the treatment process or the treatment center; they are *not recovering*.

Complainers are looking for some diversion away from what they are supposed to be working on in treatment. They may be negative about a counselor, living quarters, food, another patient, etc. Do not become emotionally involved with these negative people; it will impede your healthy recovery. You are only in treatment for a limited time, so pay attention to what is going on. Don't find love, anger, hate, disappointment, rebellion or anxiety; there is enough of this waiting for you on the outside.

Compliance and Surrender

These two little words are the key to recovery. Without these two words in your life, you have no chance of profiting from a treatment experience. You will hear these two words again in your journey. Unfortunately, Addiction seems to keep us from accepting compliance or surrender. If you have entered inpatient treatment it may help you to note and observe other patients dealing with a dangerous lack of understanding these two words. Some of the indicators are:

1. A patient will always have a criticism for events in the center. Some will make suggestions about "how" a group should be offered. He knows the "best way."

2. Some patients do their work like mechanics. These patients will claim, "I am on Step Six!!" as if speed of going through a twelve-step program is some kind of race. So we all know, some patients may take six months just accepting the first step. There is no race, no timetable, and no deadline. Recovery is a lifetime commitment. Take it easy.

3. At the end of the first month, the counselors may advise that they feel that the patient has not progressed enough to be discharged and recommend an additional month or two. Many times, the patient will state that "he has to go home" or he has "too much responsibility!" Just about all the time, this patient will go ahead and be discharged and relapse within two weeks. The conclusion is that these substance abusers are exactly the ones that should stay in treatment longer. Counselors can see when a patient needs more work.

4. When I use the word surrender and compliance, I am referring to the concept of paying attention in treatment and complying with the treatment modalities. The point is that we, as addicts, were not

COMPLIANCE AND SURRENDER

making very good decisions and that someone else is going to be in charge of my day for a period of time if I want to recover. If you are not sure what compliance and surrender mean, then you should stay in treatment until you do.

The key to recovery is surrender. This means one has to abandon their ego. This may be hard to understand. But ego is at the heart of addiction. Every treatment protocol, outpatient, MAT, AA, NA, all of them begin with a surrender of one's ego. Ego is what fueled our addiction, and ego will again fuel a relapse.

A person's ego contributes to unhealthy thinking. Beliefs such as thinking you are special and not like everyone else. Thinking that you can use "one more day" before quitting forever, that you can control your addiction, and that "using one more time" will be okay, are the results of ego run wild.

An addict's behavior is far from special. In most instances, addicts all act the same. They all lie, and in particular, lie to themselves. They all have to support their habits; therefore, they have to score money. When it comes to obtaining money, all values, faith, self-esteem, and positives are forgotten. Borrowing money that will never be repaid, stealing jewelry to pawn, and prostitution (both male and female) are all part of the addict's lifestyle.

The point of surrender is when the individual decides to "give up" what they are doing and believing and begin to listen to someone else for guidance. Their own decisions landed them in deep trouble, so they have to accept a power greater than themselves and allow this outside power to control their lives.

The process of surrender and becoming compliant is not an easy transition, and until one experiences it, there is no way to describe it. The only way I know to define this awakening is that there is a certain peace that comes with it. Recovered addicts/alcoholics will tell you that this event sometimes happens quickly, and sometimes it happens slowly. Personally, it took me years to understand and experience.

Once a person reaches this awakening about the destructive force of their ego and begins to abandon it, there is a life changing moment. In some cases, patients are so far away from understanding surrender that the best they can do is simply comply.

I think compliance to a program is the first step in recovery, particularly when one does not understand what "surrender" means. AA refers to this as "fake it, till you make it." Compliance is when the addicted decides to listen and do what he is told while in treatment or group. Recovery will work if one is compliant.

Of course, the hard drug addict, particularly the ones twenty-five years of age and younger, will struggle with both compliance and surrender. Many of them have been in several treatment centers in the past, so they have a clear picture of what the counselors are trying to do. A hard drug addict has the biggest relapse rate and generally gets very little out of treatment. The "lure" of these hard drugs, like heroin, is too powerful. Sometimes they are getting euphoria from relishing the past experiences of getting "high."

Frankly, I am not sure that words, threats, prison, health warnings, friends dying from overdose, are powerful enough dangers to curtail using hard drugs. Heroin, Cocaine, and Methamphetamine are just too strong.

One very powerful tendency in many patients who are hard drug addicts is an attitude in treatment that the center or the counselors are going to "fix" the patient. The more experienced patients who have been in multiple centers seem to have an attitude of sitting peacefully in their chairs in hopes that the protocols and treatment process will sort of "save them." For these patients, there is little hope since each patient has to be very involved in their own recovery. No one is going to save them, unless they realize that they have to "save themselves." Counselors work like crazy to penetrate the resistance in this type of patient. Usually the counselor realizes that they are working harder for the recovery of the patient than the patient is. Often the counselor will realize some futility and begin to "give up."

When counselors are working harder than the patients, it is referred to as "dancing." This comment implies that the counselor is dancing around the uninterested patient trying to penetrate his resistance. This "dance" will not work very often and alters the expectation of the patient. Patients will move from being in the "save me" mode to the "entertain me" mode. Recovery in treatment requires *work* and *commitment*. The patient will never be "saved" or "entertained" towards personal recovery. Recovery requires work and effort and understanding.

Section 2

Addiction Aspects

Medically Assisted Treatment

Naltrexone and Buprenorphine (Suboxone) are newly emerged drugs used to aid patients with opioid or alcohol addiction. They are receptor antagonists which, taken following ten days of detox, can be administered to alcoholic and opioid addicts. This has the effect of denying the patient any feelings of euphoria or "high" from drinking alcohol or using opioids.

While these drugs are not new, they are more frequently used with patients that struggle with sobriety utilizing the "normal" methods of treatment. The most single positive is that it enables patients to be self-driven in life rather than drug driven. The unique prospect of this protocol is the fact that a patient cannot truly relapse while this drug is being administered. The patient can use opioids or drink alcohol and there will be NO effect at all. Cravings are also reduced.

Suboxone, a drug containing both Buprenorphine and Naltrexone, can be used long term with no known negative serious side effects and does not require a long titration at the end of treatment. Of critical importance is the need for accompanying group and individual therapy weekly, to aid the patient in adapting to a substance free live, and in adapting to a brand new healthy lifestyle. So Suboxone and therapy are the required protocol in medically assisted treatment. It is best to discuss the entire program with a treatment professional who will design an individual treatment plan for each patient.

Some of the positives of this treatment protocol include some significant departures from the traditional protocols in the marketplace today. Specifically, these are:

1. Patient does not have to make any particular declaration, such as admitting that they are an addict or an alcoholic. The treatment is confidential.

2. One's life is no longer substance driven, and each day is not focused on obtaining the substance of choice. Life becomes Self-Driven. The medicines offer periods of time for the alcoholic or opioid addict that are not spent in obtaining more of the substance, or being somewhat "stoned" for large portions of the day and night. As the treatment continues, the patient starts to learn other means of entertaining themselves and spending time in more positive pursuits. The patient soon recognizes and begins to appreciate a new lifestyle, without the temptation or cravings to use substances. This appreciation is a very positive occurrence in this treatment protocol.

3. Treatment, if necessary, is initiated in ten days after detox, so life becomes altered in just a few days. Therapy aids the patient in adapting to a sober life.

4. There is no relapse. I have patients that were alcoholics who go with their friends to sporting events and drink a few beers with no intoxication. Abstinence is not required, although it is the goal of the program.

5. There is no money or time or stigma resulting from a thirty-day stay at an expensive treatment center. The cost of this treatment for a year is about one third of a thirty day in patient treatment experience.

6. The patient's life is not interrupted by a "disappearance" to a treatment facility of any type. Work, productivity, schoolwork, athletics, and play can go on uninterrupted. This is particularly important for people working at jobs and adolescents in high school or high school sports. Suboxone also reduces cravings for opioids and alcohol.

Regular and consistent counseling is a very important part of this protocol. The patient will encounter a complete change in lifestyle. Friends that are substance abusers will drift away, and new friends will arrive. Often the old friends return when the substance is no longer active in the patient. Also, lifestyle will change for sure. The patient will learn to adapt to a day without the time-filing events of using. Most of these positives will occur naturally but will be adjustments that need to be processed with the help of group or individual counseling. The complete medically assisted treatment program will always include regular therapy sessions to aid in adapting to a substance free lifestyle. Also the patient will benefit greatly from attending group sessions of AA or NA.

One word of warning. These drugs used for Medically Assisted Treatment work only for opioids and alcohol. Often the true "addict" will find other means of "getting high." The addict, as opposed to the addicted, is discussed in a separate chapter. The addict in MAT may find other ways to get loaded. While alcohol and opioids provide no euphoria, marijuana, Benzos, and many other drugs remain effective, so the addict can still get "high," just not on opioids or alcohol. So a person could be a patient in medically assisted therapy and be smoking pot all day long. This is why a urine analysis (UA) is also randomly administered along the way. The protocol does not permit using other drugs, and a patient that is using alternate methods of intoxication may be ejected from the program.

Many people in the treatment industry are opposed to MAT and claim that it is substituting one drug for another. I suppose that is true to some extent, but considering the relapse rate with opioids, MAT might be a lifesaving compromise. The industry is also opposed to MAT assumedly for the reason that it makes in-patient treatment centers obsolete.

Stress Affects Your Body

Understanding the mechanics of stress gives you the advantage of being more aware of and sensitive to your own level of stress and knowing when and how to take proactive steps. This increased awareness also helps you to better care for your family, friends, and colleagues. Here are a few stress facts that many people are unaware of:

Fact #1: Your Body Doesn't Care if It's a Big Stress or a Little One

The human body doesn't discriminate between a BIG stress and a little one. Regardless of the significance, stress affects the body in predictable ways. A typical stress reaction, which most of us experience dozens of times each day, begins with a cascade of 1,400 biochemical events in your body. If these reactions are left unchecked, we age prematurely, our cognitive function is impaired, our energy is drained, and we are robbed of our effectiveness and clarity.

Fact #2: Stress Can Make Smart People Do Stupid Things

Stress causes what brain researchers call "cortical inhibition." The phenomenon of cortical inhibition helps to explain why smart people do dumb things. Simply said, stress inhibits a small part of your brain, and you can't function at your best. When we are in coherence – a state where we are cognitively sharp, emotionally calm, and we feel and think with enhanced clarity – the brain, heart, and nervous system are working in harmony. This state of coherence facilitates our cognitive functioning— we are actually operating at peak performance mentally, emotionally, and physically.

Fact #3: People Can Become Numb to Their Stress

We can be physiologically experiencing stress yet mentally numb to it because we've become so accustomed to it. Some have become so adapted to the daily pressures, irritations, and annoyances of life that it starts to seem normal. Yet the small stresses accumulate quickly, and we may not realize how much they're impairing our mental and emotional clarity and our overall health until it shows up as a bad decision, an overreaction, or an unwanted diagnosis at the doctor's office.

Fact # 4: The Body and Mind Alter Depending on the Type of Stress or Anxiety Present

Actually, there are levels of anxiety. The beginning level is in the striated muscles of the body. This is the level of stress that most of us feel every day. When we are hurrying to an appointment, getting ready for work, or getting the kids ready for school early in the morning, this striated muscle level is present. Some of the physical signs of this stress level are sweating, sighing, and some motion changes. The next level is what is called smooth muscle anxiety. The smooth muscles are surrounding the arteries, in our midsection, and various parts of the body. Stress at this level can cause stomach pain, high blood pressure, migraine headaches, back pain, or pain in any part of the human body. The highest level of anxiety is called cognitive/perceptual, and results in a mental loss of reality, a panic attack, or having to ask people what they just said, and a general disconnect with the outside world.

In most cases, we do not normally recognize these levels of stress and anxiety but experience the physical results and often visit the doctor again for some cure to these symptoms. Without working on the cause of the physical presentations, we are usually wasting our time. This is why doctors often resort to prescribing an addictive benzodiazepam, such as Xanax, or Valium. These medicines reduce anxiety and stress in the body, so they are sort of dulling the cause and reduce the symptom. The problem with these drugs is that they work on the short term but never truly address the cause of the stress or anxiety. They are also addictive, and some of them, like Xanax, bind to the cells in the central nervous system and can take as much as twelve months to totally detox. In some therapeutic protocol, the counselor is quietly measuring the physical presentations of anxiety and using this crucible to determine the relative impact of the topic under discussion. The higher the level of physical events, the heavier the influence on the persons psyche. Sometimes, a trained observer can see the flexible anxiety physical events, when patients evolve from striated, to smooth, to cognitive perceptual levels.

Fact # 5: It Is Important to Note that Anxiety and Stress Are Part of Life

We all have some level of it. Anxiety is a prime motivator for everyone. Sometimes it is the motivator to work harder, play harder, have more energy, and a desire to accomplish. If we had no stress, we might not even get up to eat lunch, or even go to work, or decide to do anything. I guess we would just sit like a big pumpkin and let everything happen around us. Anxiety is fine until it gets out of control.

I tell my patients that we all have some kind of a Stress bucket somewhere in our midsection. In German, this would be called the "angsteiffel." If there is anything such as a normal person, this angsteiffel is only a little bit full. When something happens that increases anxiety or stress, this "normal" person usually does not react emotionally. The addition of a quantity to the stress bucket, because it is almost empty to start with, yields no mental or physical reaction. Most people in treatment, and for sure addicts, live each day with the stress bucket almost full. When something happens to them that adds more to the bucket, they absolutely react both mentally and physically. This can be a "blow up" or a panic attack, or some irrational and emotional reaction. The stress level can easily reach the cognitive/perceptual level, when the patient is outside the realm of reality.

The goal in treatment is to reduce the level of the stress bucket, so it is not on the brink of overflowing during the day.

In reducing the anxiety levels, we can say that anxiety is curable and treatable. Most of anxiety treatment is examining the issues that fuel the levels in the bucket, as well as conditioning the patient in physical control and relaxation. The addict that is using drugs or alcohol daily is trying to self-medicate these feelings of stress and anxiety. In most cases, the stress we all feel every day as a motivator becomes a condition of anxiety. The panic attack is the result of the Stress Bucket overflowing and cognitive/perceptual levels. Clearly, when the attack occurs, neither thinking (cognitive), nor perceptual (reality) exist for the patient.

So, this is an overview of the issues of stress and anxiety. Treatment centers attempt to reduce these levels, but can fail due to the fact that the patient might not receive enough analysis or one-on-one focused treatment. Often therapists fail to realize that addressing anxiety and reducing stress is an art form and requires some innate skills. Most importantly, this type of personal therapy cannot be learned from a class or a book. The therapist must be able to focus on the patient, not the established protocol, determine some causes of the malady through the patient's mental and physical responses, and process each cause separately.

Therapists use stress or anxiety levels portrayed by the patient to develop a focus on key life issues. As the patient charts levels of stress, namely Striated muscle, to Smooth muscle, to Cognitive Perceptual symptoms, the highest levels of anxiety cue the treatment to focus on the issues that create the highest symptom response.

Boredom

NOT TOO MANY YEARS ago, in America and elsewhere, people worked during the day. Planting, hunting, and foraging to provide shelter and sustenance. They began the day at dawn and mostly ended the workday when it was dark. Some had candlelight and most all had a fire or a fireplace. A stimulating event might be killing or capturing a large animal for meat.

Entertainment was unheard of. There was no radio, no television, no cell-phones, and no video games, just the fire to watch and provide warmth in the evening. I think that once in a while, the neighbors would all get together and do things like barn dances and things like that? I suspect that people actually talked to one another.

Then something happened: the Industrial Revolution. All of a sudden, people worked during the day in factories, earned money, and went home. Electricity illuminated everything, and in years to follow, connected everyone by phone, television, cell phone, the Internet, etc. Entertainment of all types flourished.

Music electrically reproduced, movies, television, texting, videos, and a thousand million selections to entertain everyone. The stimuli of most every person grew from an exciting day of hunting an animal for food to a million selections of entertainment. The most amazing thing is that one does not have to seek entertainment; it comes to you.

Almost all of these newly emerging methods of entertainment required us to sit still to listen and/or watch. So we sat with the attitude of "Please entertain me, we are waiting!" More and more we gradually shed the responsibility of knowing how to entertain ourselves. In the last fifty years, mankind became stimulation crazy. Everyone began reaching outside their bodies for something that would make them happy on the inside.

Clothing, automobiles, designer this, designer that, special tennis shoes, golf clubs, hats, fancier cell phones, the list is endless. Some might say, "Well, this is progress!" Maybe it is progress, but the world of provision, that is, a world that provides us with things to stimulate us, is moving much faster than evolution.

Man has sort of been left behind emotionally and spiritually.

When you look at your children and see them totally engaged in the use of a cell phone or small computer, note how much they are entertaining themselves. Tell them to put the phone away and that the entire family is going to build a fire in the backyard and sit around it and talk.

See how far you can get with that idea, and you will see what I am talking about. Simply, without all of these entertainment modules like cell phones, computers, etc., everyone is bored.

There are many kinds of boredom, and clinician's debate over the source and impact of boredom on man. The main thing to remember is that we are conditioned to heavy stimuli, and our society has become accustomed to being entertained most of the day. When the stimuli are removed for even a short period, boredom arrives.

Boredom, I believe, is the most influential factor in modern day human addiction. My wonderful mentor, Bonnie Dendooven is the leading proponent in America of the influence of boredom on addiction, and most importantly, boredom causing relapse after treatment. To my knowledge, she is the only entity researching boredom and treating boredom today in a clinical research/treatment setting.

I think it is accurate to include alcohol, nicotine, drugs of all type, and any substance of abuse as *entertainment*. Substances of abuse provide a stimulus to many. An example is going to a concert, or going to a concert stoned. The latter is some kind of "value added" entertainment. This added value is probably not positive. The problem with drugs being entertainment is that the ones that work the best are the most addictive and can morph into full-blown physiological, spiritual, and psychological dependencies.

Did people on the frontier get bored with life? I have no idea. I am not sure if they had the time to get bored. Today, however, boredom is commonplace. I am not talking here about the kind of boredom that one feels when they are waiting for a plane flight. I am talking about what happens when people who have a problem with substances do when boredom sets in. Frankly, I believe it is the number one reason for relapse after a treatment program. The addict does not know how to deal with boredom, without using substances. They do not know what to do with their *time*. Boredom raises their anxiety levels, makes them edgy, and drives them nuts. The addict knows that the one simple solution to boredom is alcohol or drugs.

Substances really help pass the time quickly. Youths who bore easily, are not involved in extracurricular activities in school, and tend to isolate are prime candidates for drug or alcohol abuse. The first "experiment" with drugs or alcohol will be a transcending moment, when all of these problems and negatives dissolve into euphoria. Unfortunately, HEROIN is the champion of euphoria, and is more than likely available in your area. If you believe you are immune from hard drug distribution because you are in the suburbs or "small-town USA" you are mistaken. America is approaching saturation.

Addiction, Boredom, and Anxiety are all co-existing in the addictive personality. If one increases, they all increase independently. The addict when bored is nervous. The addict when bored wants some relief. The addicts mind tells the person to self-medicate. Boredom is the enemy of recovery.

As a solution to Boredom, never let the person isolate. Oddly, when an addict becomes bored or lonely, they feel that best answer to this is isolation. They will go into their room, get under the covers and just dial out of the day. You will see this for sure if you have an addict at home. Obviously, the response of isolation to a condition of loneliness or boredom is pretty ridiculous. This response usually makes the issue worse, not better. Today, people isolate with their phones. If you can, keep them moving, give them projects, work, and play, whatever. The most successful recoveries are not people in isolation, they are people who work a full schedule, eat well, get plenty of rest, exercise, and attend regular meetings.

Meetings can be daily if needed. My point is there are *always* activities that can fill a day up. Sometimes the addict is *unable* to manage his/her time well, and needs coaching. If one is idle and bored, the next step will be relapse.

The successful addict in recovery will probably have a schedule full of daily activities. Idle time becomes a period of rest and relaxation, not a period of boredom.

Typical Day:

- Wake
- Shower and Shine

- Go to work
- Go to recovery meeting
- Go to gym and follow regimen
- Prepare an evening meal
- Complete personal chores—pay bills, laundry, clean house, etc.
- Make healthy plans for the weekend

Note that with this kind of daily regimen there is little time to be bored.

One very important issue as it relates to the *Treatment Talk* topic, is that *no treatment* protocols exist to diagnose and treat boredom. Currently, to my knowledge, there is one researcher in the country working on this malady from a therapeutic standpoint, Bonnie Dendooven. So, when someone goes into treatment as an inpatient or an outpatient, they will receive no aid in fighting boredom or even any methods to reduce it. Some believe that the number one cause of relapse is the anxiety/boredom syndrome. People go home from treatment, are extremely bored, develop added anxiety, and self-medicate with the drug of choice. Remember that the number one goal of treatment is to prevent relapse, yet boredom is not addressed in any manner.

If you have a loved one living with you that is *not* practicing living in the numbered events on the previous page, they are more than likely setting themselves up for relapse. All of these eight daily functions are centered on self-reliance and discipline. Unfortunately, all addicts are usually afflicted with high levels of defiance. They often want to do everything "their way" rather than following a regimen not of their design. Defiance will be dealt with in later chapters, and could be the coconspirator in developing addiction.

Defiance

Addiction, by nature, is defiance. Every addict is defiant, particularly the more substance used, the greater the defiance. Addicts are automatically afflicted with the self-confidence that they are absolutely right and correct all the time. They feel they know how to control their problem; they think they can quit anytime they want to and believe the outside world has no understanding of any of their struggles. They are egomaniacs with low self-esteem.

When entering treatment of any kind, there is a tendency on the part of the patient to modify any treatment program, adopting the attitude of "I'll show you" rather than "I need help." The act of defiance itself is never fully understood by the abuser. They feel strongly that they have the best practices. Most can never come to the realization that in treatment protocols, such as Alcoholics Anonymous, and its hundred years of existence, just about everything has been tried. What remains is the path that works. The rules and approaches in AA work if the patient is willing to work it. Some general components of successful recovery are:

- Read material—all programs have some special literature, AA has the "Big Book."
- Don't do it alone—usually there are meetings and one needs a "sponsor." Recovery will not work on your own.
- Be consistent—each program will have a group of challenges in order. Conquer them fully and one at a time.
- Compliance—utilizes all the program components; do not pick and choose. The addict will fail if he tries to design his own program.
- Persistence—is willing to recover and if there is a relapse, return to recovery. Accept relapse as a stage of recovery.

The main problem for the addict is that they cannot self-realize that they are being defiant with no real purpose or intent. They just want to do things their own way. Patients who have been in several treatment centers, worked some aftercare, then relapsed, are no more accepting of the fact that their defiance made them fail. Even when therapists or peers challenge them with comments such as, "Hey how did *your* program work for you the last time?" they still remain objectionable to the formula for success, even though their "program" led to a fast relapse upon release.

Underneath in the addict's psyche, there is always bubbling this tendency to defy, to be self-determined, to be original, to be overly prideful. Defiance is a danger point for relapse, and it often goes unrecognized and untreated. To my knowledge no treatment centers truly deal with this affliction.

Most addicts are bright and creative; many approach genius levels in some categories. However, the level of defiance is sometimes so high that their talent is never recognized in the school systems, as they portray the "rebel." Although defiance can be an ongoing problem, by itself it may not cause relapse. What intensifies Defiance is when Defiance arrives with its cruel stepsister, *boredom*. The conditions of defiance, loneliness, and boredom combined are primary to Relapse.

Remember, in treatment centers, Defiance is never treated as a separate malady, and neither is Boredom. When Boredom comes in on top of Defiance, the addict is more than likely going to find their favorite substance and use. Imagine a personality that is self-centered to the point of listening to their own solitary drummer day and night, and add that anxiety that is created, the restlessness, of being bored. Unfortunately, in treatment, there is a lot of free time, and doing things that the addict probably deems ridiculous, repetitive, or unworthy of their participation. Boredom multiplied by Defiance. This is what causes all addicts, and particularly adolescents, to use alcohol and drugs. It is a simple formula, a simple causative, but very difficult to isolate and treat.

Patients in treatment centers, and those that have been in treatment from a couple of months, will always state that "I am bored with treatment." When asked what is boring to them, they will respond "going to group, meetings, group, meetings, group, etc." Yet when these same patients are asked, "What exactly have you learned or experienced here in treatment?" they will never state these various coping mechanisms they have been taught, discussed, processed, and experienced every day. They are "bored" because they have failed to engage, or are failing to engage any longer in the treatment process. This same group of patients that struggle with stating or recognizing any positive learning or healing experiences have all been treated with:

- Relaxation Therapy—methods to relax, control, reduce, and process anxiety.
- Tips, Tools, and Techniques—all designed to redirect energy from using to living a drug free life.
- Communications—methods of being assertive rather than being aggressive. Anger Management.
- Living—adapting to roommates and group living. Concern for others.
- Higher Power—surrendering life events to anyone other than yourself, since your decisions were not too positive for you.
- Cognitive Behavioral Therapy—altering learned thoughts and behaviors as responses.

Every course of treatment will contain some or all of these protocols and methods every single day. If a patient is unable to mention one or two of these as being part of his/her experience, then they have truly missed the intent of treatment. They are not bored, they have just disengaged in the process. The more they are listening to their addictive voices and defiance, the more bored they will be.

Most counselors never mention that Defiance is a source of, or at least a powerful component of, *addiction*. I think it is the great power that begins, sustains, and relapses addicts. There are even tests available today that will measure the level of defiance in an elementary school child, as being some kind of an indicator measuring the potential of future addictive behavior.

I suppose it is nice to know, or maybe frightening, to know about the hypothetical future of our children, and to know if they have a propensity towards addiction.

The problem as I see it is that if one tests for a high propensity for substance use and abuse at age eight, what can we do about it? Kids certainly do not understand logic. Oftentimes, the level of understanding in a child is challenged just learning what "no" means. Now, we are supposed to think that we can say, "Oh my goodness, you have tested really high on defiance scales, you have to stop that or you might be an addict?" Not sure that we would get too far with this in child raising.

What might be really helpful to us, however, is that we *recognize defiance* in our children, our spouses, our coworkers, our friends, and the addicts we know. Once we begin to see defiant behavior around us, it just seems to be very, very visible all of a sudden. Do not confuse Defiance with Rebelliousness; there is a difference. The Hells Angels, as an example, could be defined as rebels, as their dress, language and behavior is not "normal" in American society. However, a member will not appear to be a "rebel" within the group. One can still be a member of the Hells Angels and be Defiant within the group.

Let's look at some symptoms of defiance in our daily lives. The more we can recognize the symptom, the more we begin to understand, and maybe we can redirect it.

Example 1—someone wants a big chocolate donut. It is all they can think about. They are overweight, and they have eaten a meal recently, so they are not truly hungry, or starving. The doctor has warned them about their insulin levels, and advised *not* to eat sugar at *all*. They were told to lose weight, cut back on carbs, etc. We have all received doctor's directions from time to time. The subject is mentally focused on this delicious frosted chocolate donut at the shop down the street. It is just a few feet away, easy walking distance. All of a sudden, they rise from their chair, walk to the donut, buy the donut and eat every crumb of it! I have personal experience with this particular action, and will confess that if one eats no sugar for a few days, this donut, filled with sugar, fat, and carbs does not just taste good. It tastes *fabulous*. I will also confess that after eating the donut, there is a slight, maybe very slight feeling of guilt, remorse, and maybe even regret.

Remember sugar is one of those substances that we look for, on the outside of our bodies, and think that by bringing it "into our bodies "that the substance will make us feel better. If you don't believe this, please visit an ice cream shop and notice how many people are smiling and laughing. Sugar works, and it works well for a while. Insulin boost at first then declines in a couple of hours or so. Sugar makes you feel energized and happy for a while, then tired and deflated later. Many consider sugar an addictive substance as well.

Okay, we are not on a path to condemn sugar, but begin to understand the power of defiance. Here are the steps that were involved in the chocolate donut splurge.

- First, the thought of the big frosted chocolate donut comes to mind.
- Second, it just really sounds good to eat one. We can almost smell it.
- Third, we hold off, thinking of the doctor's warning, and our own personal pledge not to have sugar.
- Fourth, we start thinking that we have not had any sugar for two weeks, and that is pretty good!
- Fifth, we then tell ourselves, "it's okay to splurge once in a while." In fact, I remember the doctor saying that it's "okay to have a piece of pie on Thanksgiving, or Birthday cake, once in a while."
- Sixth, that's it! We get out of the chair and start the walk to the shop.

Nothing can change our mind now, nothing can stop us. Nothing *will* stop us.

Does this silly little example sound familiar? I am sure it does. We have all done something like this. Oddly, these are the same justifying thoughts that surface in an addict's mind when faced with the temptation of using.

As mentioned before, relapse is a *process* in the addict's thinking. Defiance and Boredom aid in the process of relapse. If a patient was equipped to recognize and alter most of these preliminary thought processes, we might be able to reduce relapse rates. Unfortunately, no treatment facilities diagnose or treat levels of boredom or defiance.

Example 2—This example might be called the "I have a better idea" friend. We all have these types of friends, and they are frustrating. Here is what they do:

- No matter what restaurant is suggested, they want to change it.
- No matter what departure time is suggested, they want to change it.
- No matter what movie is suggested as entertainment, they want to change it.
- No matter what comical story is shared, they always add one they think if more comical.

DEFIANCE

Okay, I think you see where I am going here in my explanations. The problem with defiance in substance abusers is that these levels of self-indulgence and satisfaction are operating at very high levels, even though the thinking and actions are self-destructive. The addict will justify using or drinking with a series of justifications, fueled by Defiance. In contrast to a chocolate donut, however, the decision to use or drink can be fatal. This decision is the prelude to overdose and overdose death.

Section 3

Treatment Talk

Cell Phones

I think just about all therapists hate cell phones. The Apple iPhone hit the market in the summer of 2007. I have heard statements that there are over 2 billion of these cell phones in use in the world. Realize that these phones have become almost like an extra "arm" to most people. While dining with my wife of 45 years, we noticed a couple about our ages eating in silence. They never said a word to each other, and every few minutes, they would reach in their pockets or purse and check their individual phones! I was hoping they were not texting each other, rather than just talking, but one never knows. Amazing how these devices have penetrated our lives in about eleven years.

Treatment centers vary in their policies of allowing cell phone use. Some prohibit them altogether, some permit certain time of day use, and others only require them to be off when the patient is in a group, educational lecture, or individual therapy.

Emerging in the psychological/psychiatric world is the view that cell phones and the use of them is an *addiction*. Remember the statement that claimed that addictive behavior is when someone looks outside for something they can bring inside to make him or her feel better. So in addition to alcohol, drugs, sex, food, gambling, etc. we have added the cell phone. The use of cell phones, connecting with the world, is a process that produces emotions, feelings of good or bad, and entertainment. For many people, these little electronic devices have become instrumental in daily life. I was lecturing at a major university and was in an elevator filled with students. All of them were glued to cell phones. I always like to make jokes and comments, so I asked them all, "Hey! Let's try something new! Why don't you all put away your cell phones, talk and get to know each other?" The reaction was astounding! They all just looked at me and . . . laughed!

I am not sure if any psychologist or social psychologist can truly measure the emotional impact of these devices. For many, the cell phone is a special little communication and fantasy world that removes one from their surroundings. This world is a separate one from what is happening in the room, the restaurant, the dinner table, studying, and addiction treatment. Unquestionably, when a person is "cell phoning" they are:

- Isolated
- Stimulated
- Unfocused
- Private
- Emotionally involved
- Entertained
- Reclusive
- Unreachable

Look back over these co-occurring conditions yielded by cell phone use. Note that *all* of these conditions are the *same* as when one is using drugs or alcohol. All of these apply to a person who is abusing substances.

In treatment, these are exactly the traits we are trying to defeat. Each mental status is a prelude to having an urge to *use*. When a patient fires up their cell phones, they might as well be on Mars than in a group session. They are unreachable and unfocused, unteachable and zoned out. They are *gone*.

Sometimes I think it is harder to take a cell phone away from a patient, than taking alcohol or drugs away. Certainly the electronics are an addiction, and I would believe that inpatient treatment should remove all forms of entertainment and connection with the outside world. Removing cell phones from addicts requires a crowbar.

There are many instances of patients walking out of treatment centers when told they cannot have a cell phone for a month. The cell phone is often more important to the individual than recovery. In treatment, the cell phone can be a dangerous entity. Relationships can be developed through texts, as well as ordering drugs on line. Yes, drugs can be delivered if you know the right phone number. Simply, the phone is a distraction from recovery. The treatment industry is caught in a bind, since few patients would "check in" to centers that did not allow cell phones. So, the treatment business, already dealing with a new, drug addicted patient, is trapped into allowing residents to keep their phones, further deterring the already ineffective treatment process.

I wonder years from now, if someone asks one of these students whether or not they enjoyed attending this university, they may very well respond that "it was a little boring." Yes it was a little boring, because the students "missed" part of the college experience. I fully realize that I am considered old fashion, but most of my patients in treatment are much more engaged with cell phone use than in learning anything in treatment.

I have watched patients during individual sessions, when their phone goes "ping" in their pockets. When the "ping" sounds, we might as well end the therapy session, because all the patient can think of is, "What's on my phone?" The patient is obsessed with wondering who is texting? "Is it the girl that I met and texted this morning?" These texts create an emotional response. The response could be positive or negative, but the texts have emotion tied to them. In a treatment environment, particularly at full time inpatient, these little phones are a constant connection to the outside world, and the outside world is exactly what we are trying to isolate the patient from. We are trying to communicate, help, and treat the patient in a protected environment void of outside influences. With the arrival of a text, the safety, direction, progress, and isolation from outside disappears.

Outside relationships, loves, friends, circumstances, and events now appear magically in the treatment session. The therapist is now ignored and something from the outside has entered into the consciousness of the recovering patient. I hate cell phones. I have seen studies and commentaries about how many hours the average person spends watching television. In the past, psychologists were commenting about the isolating effect of the "tube."

Today, we have not only television, but the addition of the cell phone, computers on the internet, and instant connection with people, companies, sports, the "news," Facebook, Snapchat, Tweets, texting, and I don't know of how many forms of communication and entertainment. I have personally experienced parts of these new methods. I remember going to the library, going through the millions of cards to locate a book or journal article as an adjunct to the subject of interest. Today, one can instantly have all the article options, with summaries and evaluations, in front of one's eyes in seconds. I would hope that the Internet has *improved* education at all levels.

The Psychiatry Industry uses a manual, called the DSM-V, to identify and classify mental illnesses. Addiction is well defined and categorized in the publication. The current version includes electronic participations of all sorts. The DSM-V is the "go to" manual for diagnosing psychiatric and behavioral illnesses, providing a code for each malady so that insurance companies will clearly understand and subsidize the treatment. In the next version, the DSM-VI, cell phones, gaming, and audiovisual addiction will be clearly defined and categorized as a mental illness and obsession.

If you don't believe that these programs and devices are addictive, take your child's cell phone away from them and see if they can go a day without a cell phone, video games, internet, etc. They will seriously go into some kind of withdrawal. Try this and you will see what I mean. We have a serious addiction going on right under our noses. I realize that I am biased, however. I have treated what might be called "hard core" drug addicts and every one of them presents with multiple addictions. Smoking cigarettes or vaping, cell phones, and obsessive relationships are all a powerful part of the addict's lifestyle.

If you are paying all the money to send a friend or a loved one to ipatient treatment, I promise that they will be better served with *all contact with the outside world eliminated*. A treatment center that allows cell phone use is just kidding themselves at providing effective treatment protocols.

So I am clear about electronics, cell phones, games, the Internet, etc. are *addictive*. They provide a special stimulus to individuals who are, indeed, self-medicating with drugs or alcohol.

Researchers are just beginning to understand this type of addiction, as electronics are relatively new. The future will evaluate the impact of all these electronic influences and produce treatment protocols to address these modern day and unique addictions. All of these issues with electronic dependencies and addiction are bubbling in the mental health field. I am sure there will be many cascading articles about the use and abuse of electronics. We are in the middle of the storm.

In most of our homes with adolescents or any youthful person, we can expect to have them "glued" to their electronics. We don't have youngsters at home anymore, but I assume that even the active high school "jock" tends to utilize daily electronics. Most kids spend hours in the electronic world. You can easily spot the ones who are probably developing a dependency or maybe even an addiction to electronics.

So you might ask, "How is this relevant to treatment centers?" Picture a young person addicted to black tar heroin and dependent upon cell phone and the Internet. Today's treatments will try to address this complex youth with protocols adapted from Alcoholics Anonymous and methodologies from the 1990s. I understand that treatment professionals in the centers today will say that I am totally wrong and don't know what I am talking about. Maybe I don't, but the *results* of today's centers are so pathetic that I feel pretty strongly that they are not utilizing inventive and helpful methods or "cures." I have seen the comments and blank stares from patients addicted to heroin plus other hard drugs when treatment staff says "Hey, we are going to an AA meeting tonight!" Treatment is missing the mark.

Of interest is the fact that when some people arrive at the treatment center and the staff informs them that they have to surrender their cell phone, the patient will just simply turn around and leave. I suspect that if a center, treating patients under thirty, did not allow cell phone use at all, they might not have any patients! There is significant pressure to allow cell phone use on campus, even though they provide an enormous diversion to the entire process of recovery and treatment.

Cell phones that connect to the Internet and provide "handheld" entertainment are sort of new. We have had about ten years or so experience, so no one truly has any conclusions about how these devices might impact our society. These little objects provide entertainment. Drugs and alcohol also provide entertainment. Humans seek entertainment, seemingly more and more all the time.

Many years ago I worked for the great Pillsbury Company, based in Minneapolis, Indiana. I was a field salesman for all of our Grocery Products that you would be familiar with. I was in the Midwest and drove to see various customers and chain headquarters. My day would probably include a stop to use a pay phone to call the regional office each day. When the day was over, if I were out of town, I would stay in a motel and the evenings were my time. So I worked about eight hours a day or so. Today, while I am driving, I would be on my cell phone most of the time, and the evenings would be spent in my room on a laptop computer, so my actual "workday" would be more like ten or twelve hours, with no real breaks. I guess the worker is more efficient, but the leisure time is drastically reduced. Even when I was driving, listening to the radio and relaxing, the time spent was not work time. This new workday, I would have to think, is much more stressful and demanding, with extensive connectivity 24/7 and less time for one's self.

Conclusion

I hope you enjoyed and found value in this treatise. I tried to write it simply and in an easy-to-read format for this second book of the *Addiction Trilogy*.

I realize that the *solutions* are probably a little vague from time to time, and the reason for that is that there truly is no true Science of Addiction Treatment. There are hundreds of treatment protocols available, but the world of addiction, and particularly the world of hard drug addiction, has caught standard recovery counseling a little off balance. Frankly, no one was prepared for the onslaught of Meth, Cocaine, and Heroin- not the police, the schools, the communities or the treatment centers. While Meth has been around in strength for a while, Heroin is new to suburbia. The new Black Tar Heroin all comes across the border from Mexico and has been sold in strength in the USA for about five years. Heroin is not just inner city; it is in every community nationwide.

Heroin, Cocaine, and Meth are much more powerful, controlling, and dangerous than alcohol, although all substances can be fatal. The epidemic of hard drug use among our youth is at a crisis proportion and requires new and drastic measures to treat and combat. Obviously, one of the most contributing factors to hard drug use is availability. The distribution networks developed by suppliers are intricate, widespread, and difficult to attack. Low-level dealers, when apprehended by law enforcement, usually have small quantities that generate short jail time or probationary sentences. These dealers look at jail time as part of the job and accept it. Since all of the jails are crowded, most receive probationary sentences and are released back to the streets where they can go right back to work selling drugs.

Unfortunately, the federal government fails miserably in thwarting distribution, and, in fact, drugs are more available on Main Street USA today than ever before. Who would have ever thought that a substance such

CONCLUSION

as Black Tar Heroin (Black) would be available in a high school in rural America?

Most teenagers experiment with drugs today. Often at parties, strong drugs appear and the kids only have to sniff a pinch to experience the euphoria. To many, "sniffing" or "snorting" does not seem like a big deal. Many would think this action is harmless.

Perhaps this first experience IS harmless, but sometime begins a deadly cycle that leads to addiction. Today, many alcoholics are cross-addicted to alcohol and drugs.

All we can do, I suppose, is prepare our loved ones and friends and help them the best we can. That is the purpose of this book, to give us all some guidelines. I hope it helps. With the continuing failure of our current preventative measures, it may be that individuals in communities will ban together to stop drugs from being distributed and sold in their neighborhoods. The beginnings of these activist groups are just starting to sprout up in a number of communities.

One of the continuing crisis events in our nation is the fact that when addiction does hit a family, few have any idea what to do about it. The family, and particularly the adults, feel frightened and alone. Most react with instantly forcing their child to go to treatment. I hope this trilogy helps those that feel alone and lost. I hope it helps in understanding there are many kinds of treatment, and that the success of treatment is truly in the hands of the patient.

Thank you, Kent I. Phillips

The Ten Commandments of Helping

For parents that are struggling with an addicted sibling, or for anyone with an addicted friend, here is what I call the *Ten Commandments of Helping*. Clearly, most of the things that we do in the spirit of "helping" actually damage the afflicted. Here are the top ten things that we must commit to for helping the friends or relatives with a Substance Abuse Problem. I hope these help.

1. Thou shalt tell the afflicted that you stand with them in recovery, but you shall not stand with them in Addiction.
2. Thou shalt not give the Afflicted any money.
3. Your home is your domain of safety; you shall always have rules for all to abide by.
4. You shall not heed the words of the Afflicted, you will heed only actions.
5. Thou shall not provide a nest for the Addicted to live, eat, slumber, or hide.
6. Thou shalt not believe any promises of the Addicted and ignore them. Believe only *actions*.
7. Thou shalt not show love of the Addicted with gifts. Love is not presents.
8. Thou shall not feel guilt for failing. Drugs are stronger than you.
9. Recovery is not hours, days, weeks or years, it is lifelong.
10. Never confuse loving with giving or providing.

Often friends or parents feel better when they feel they are helping the substance abuser. This "help" is often in the form of money, room and board. While many would think that keeping the afflicted in your home, feeding them, clothing them, etc. is helping, in reality these provisions are actually supporting not the Addict, but the Addiction. The sooner the patient comes to the decision that using is self-destructive and develops a desire to change, the sooner serious sobriety begins. Pampering the addict just enables them to continue in a "drug life." I realize that it is difficult to stop physical help, because helping makes US feel better. Every minute, hour, or day one enables the user to survive as is the further away a sober life remains.

Many with an addicted son, daughter or another loved one are tempted to "help" them. Remember, the addict knows exactly how to play on your guilt. They are masters at using guilt to stimulate you to give them room and board, clothes and money. This guilt makes you afraid to "cut them loose" to live on their own. There is always the fear that the loved one, if cast out, will die. Yes, this is a possibility, but it is not you that caused them to die. Harboring them can also help them to take an overdose and die as well. For those using hard drugs daily, death is always just around the corner. Taking care of their needs will only lengthen the addiction; you have no control over the loved one overdosing or meeting some evil fate on the streets.

BOOK 3

KILLING FAMILY

To the Reader

THIS BOOK IS NOT written for the clinical professional, it is written for the people experiencing addiction of a loved one or friend. For those who need some source, providing honest and true assessments of the situation. So many parents and concerned parties are just simply lost when Addiction comes home to visit. This is not a professional treatise, nor does it follow formatting and quoting rules established by the American Psychological Association. I felt it useless to stick in source quotes to refer to research result articles or statistics. I suppose one might call this work a "layman's approach." This book is based primarily on observations and conclusions generated by my personal experience in clinical work and recovery. I hope it helps. Also, there are direct recommendations contained in this book. Before you decide to use this *trilogy* as your guideline for dealing with addiction, consult a licensed and skilled healthcare professional for actual advice and counsel regarding your specific issues. Every situation, while exhibiting a number of similarities, is always unique. Addiction Treatment and Handling is never a "one size fits all" approach. Always get help.

Also deserving recognition is Bill O'Reilly, who has written great books about history called *Killing Kennedy, Killing Lincoln*, etc. These are great reads, and I recommend them highly. His books inspired the title of *Killing Family* for this work, as I believe that *Killing Family* is exactly the term best describing the impact of drugs and alcohol on our culture. I suppose a more general term, such as *Killing America*, might be just as appropriate, but thank you Bill O'Reilly!

Introduction

Adolescents experiment with drugs and alcohol; accept it. Sometimes they are arrested for experimenting, since many drugs are controlled substances. Data suggests about eighty percent of high school seniors have used a substance of some kind during high school. For almost all, using a substance is a rite of passage and a learning moment. For some, about one in ten, the initial experience is a true magical revelation. The general impression for this latter group is "I can't believe I feel this way" and "this is how I want to live." One of the temptations here is that the stronger the substance, the greater the experience. Unfortunately, the years from 12 to 21 are formative, and most adolescents experience anxiety, self-doubt, insecurity, and stress. These feelings are part of growing into an adult. The problem with using substances during these years is that THEY WORK! While in the system, drugs and alcohol provide euphoria and a relief from all of the challenging adolescent feelings. All of one's problems dissolve.

One in ten of the youthful experimenters are future addicts. More than likely, they suffer from anxiety, depression, or some mental health issue. This is not to say they are crazy, but they are struggling with some issues at a level that maybe not everyone experiences.

Their first use is a tremendous self-medicating event, and any suffering disappear with substance use. They will repeat use and navigate to other substances. Whatever the adolescent first uses will become their "gateway" drug. The probability of this adolescent using and abusing substances during youth and into maturity is very high.

Picture a young person with undiagnosed, low level anxiety, grief, or depression. Finding a substance that makes them feel "normal" for the first time. It is a fabulous discovery, a catharsis, and a breakthrough.

INTRODUCTION

Some continue to seek and experience this level of relief and begin a daily use syndrome. The problem is the fact that most of the "relief substances" are mentally and/or physiologically addictive. On the following pages you will find topics dissecting addictive behavior, the family, treatment options, and a general treatise on what one should do when a friend or family member is suffering from addiction.

Please note that this is merely a handbook, and is not medical or clinical advice. I suppose the utility of this book is to help us all live with a little less anxiety about our loved one and possibly what we can do to help him/her recover. The goal is to walk with you to move beyond denial and hopelessness to acceptance and action.

The problem is that virtually all of these substances are habit forming, require larger quantities to obtain the same results, and damage health. In some cases, too much of the substance can cause death.

The history of people over 21 years of age that abuse alcohol and/or drugs will more than likely contain early experimentations that continued on to be a regular habit. The more powerful the drug, the greater the allure. The more powerful the drug, the harder to recover. You will note in the readings that I claim that the current recovery/treatment systems are overwhelmed and fail to find curative protocols. Relapse rates on hard drugs are over 90 percent. I consider such a high relapse rate a failure of the treatment industry. This failure will be reviewed in detail, and is carried to an even more detail in the second book in this *trilogy*, entitled *Treatment Talk*.

The odds are you are reading this book because addiction has entered your home or attacked a loved one. Addiction, I am afraid, is not like other diseases. There is no cure, no remedy, and no medication. In addition, addiction has its own voice and talks to the afflicted. Addiction tells the addict to keep using, to run from treatment, and a thousand other negative messages.

With other diseases, the afflicted is uni-affected, meaning that they are the one that suffers most. With addiction, everyone around the addict suffers, sometimes without realizing it. Family hierarchies and roles are transformed, and a certain tension and shame arrives.

This book will deal with what happens to everyone when addiction comes to visit, and what you should do about it. I say to parents, siblings, relatives and friends, please take note that although much of what you will read here is opinion, the opinion is derived from fact and experience. I feel that we can all benefit from knowing what to do, when, and how to do it, to remain healthy.

I suppose that it would be realistic to think, while reading, that this book is directed towards the mothers of the afflicted. Somehow, I feel that moms are the ones that suffer most when a child or husband is swept away by substances. Moms are the ones that sit at home at night and suffer, fearing that the phone will ring, and at the same time, worrying when it doesn't.

This book is for parents who feel lost, to help you through the crisis of Addiction. Always remember, you didn't cause it, you can't control it and you can't cure it. I wish we could just sit a loved one down and logically explain to them that they are making mistakes. Unfortunately, I have learned that logic will not work. The Voices of Addiction are much louder than logic, in fact so loud that our efforts are unheard. A major component of Addiction is *defiance*. Some experts believe that a child can be evaluated for future substance abuse problems by measuring their levels of *defiance* at a young age. All addicts are defiant. Addicts are inundated with logic, from the moment that someone discovers their substance use. Friends, , relatives, police, jail, judges, all warn of the dangers. Yet the addict continues to use and abuse. Logic is ineffective.

Defiance rules. Even after spending time in a treatment center for thirty to ninety days, the afflicted begins to believe that they can "use when they want to" and that they "have it under control." Thoughts such as these, defiant and ridiculous as they are, always lead to relapse. The *voices* of Addiction tell the user that they are all powerful and in control.

America's answer to the Addiction Crisis is to open treatment centers of all types all over the nation. Treatment is big business. Treatment is expensive. Treatment is the accepted path. Many insurance plans pay for treatment. There are basic centers and very fancy ones. Some centers are even on the waterfront. Some centers use twelve step programs, hypnosis, music therapy, yoga, anxiety control, diet and exercise, spiritualism, and many protocols for treatment. So that you know, the truth is, *none of them work*. The absolute requirement for attaining sobriety is the patient's *will* to change.

Without this will to change, treatment is a waste of time. Relapse is inevitable. When the afflicted is ready to go to treatment they will say, "I can't take it anymore, I really want to change" to us; these comments are very encouraging and hopeful. In most cases, however, what the afflicted is really saying, "I am starting to feel uncomfortable, and I need a break."

INTRODUCTION

Sometimes the afflicted is in legal trouble and feels that treatment is a place to "hide out" or that treatment will help them with the judge's verdict and penalties. I have heard a number of statistics, but the most realistic one is that those that attend treatment centers and do not cultivate a post-treatment support structure have a 1 in 30 chance of staying sober.

So, a center with a hundred patients can only expect about three to attain sobriety. I suppose it would be accurate to say that treatment works if the individual has a sincere commitment to change and develops a post treatment program of group and individual support.

"This seems all so hopeless," you might say. Yes and no. No, we can't magically cure someone, we can't change him or her, we cannot control addiction, but yes, we can support the addict without *enabling* him or her to continue his or her destructive behavior. Yes, we can have the strength to aid them when they relapse. Yes, we can try to understand them, and yes, we can love them. Most importantly, we can recognize their game-like consistent behavior and hope to identify and develop a posture and attitude that is positive and productive, if not always pleasant, so that we do not make the situation worse.

For the young, remember that their problem all started with an innocent experiment. A moment of youth, that blossomed into a terrifying lifestyle. Sometimes it seems as if young addicts are victims, swept away by euphoria, a powerful subculture, and ease of availability.

One day, they turn around and realize that they are in trouble. They need us. The behavior of most addicts is a kind of "cry for help" and in some ways, we can provide that help. This third book in the *trilogy*, *Killing Family*, will examine what parents should do, and what they should not do. Each friend or relative should never think that they are showing love by providing items such as money, food, housing, etc.

Provision of this type of love to the addict is immediately converted to methods to get high. One final note: *all addicts are liars*. I know that you have trouble believing that your precious son, daughter, or friend would ever tell you a lie, but once addicted, they seem to have no choice.

This book is a *handbook* for dealing with *addiction*. I hope it helps those suffering from the arrival of addition. *Killing Family* is what *addiction* does; just never lose sight of the fact that *addiction* is the only voluntary, self-administered, and supported disease that eventually kills the afflicted.

This book is divided into three sections, each dealing with a "stage of experience" in dealing with Addiction. The first section gives a general overview of the Problem itself, and the general environment in which your addict exists. The second section deals with the "discovery" of drug or alcohol use, and/or the true level of abuse, and how to react and deal with these moments. Section three addresses the nature of the abuser and the issues leading up to Relapse, a part of normal recovery and something necessary to expect and deal with.

I have personally experienced most of the scenarios described in this book, or have had individuals sitting across from me in therapy reveal these "inside truths."

Some might ask us *"What is the solution?"* I wish I had a clear answer. Maybe the best way to cleanse our society is to reverse the events of the last four or five years. By reversing, I mean to stop the drugs coming here from Mexico, and then stop the distribution of them in our communities. This will require a social/political movement in which the citizens, the addicts, law enforcement and education all combine to fight the availability of drugs. Right now, it seems that all of these mentioned entities are blaming each other in a non-productive manner.

I hope and pray that the following treatise proves helpful to you all. I realize that much of the following is my opinions and observations, but everything is painfully true.

One more comment: addiction of a loved one is *not your fault*. Many parents fret over the fact that they divorced, and that this unpleasant event sparked addiction in our kids. *Not true.* One half of all families experience divorce, yet one half of kids are *not* addicted. No one is sure exactly what is at play in the addicted psyche, but for sure, it wasn't you.

Kent I. Phillips, MSAC, MS.
Master Addiction Specialist

SECTION 1

The Problem

The Predator

Most of America looks upon addiction as a human weakness. Some even think that one can just order someone to "snap out of it" and that will be curative. Some think that addiction is just something that happens in big cities, or that it is the sole property of the inner cities. Some think that basic love and care will cure a victim. Some fathers of addicted children feel they can just "command" a child to be clean and sober. I wish these approaches were effective, but they are not.

Some believe that a person is just born with a "bad gene" that develops into alcoholism or drug addiction. I would guess that my response to these visions is "maybe," but there are aspects of the addiction epidemic that are much more permanent and frightening.

American, we are under attack by a very large and dangerous predator. Like a virus, the predator destroys its host. Unlike a virus, this predator attacks families, religions, neighborhoods, schools, education, and our culture. This predator is *addiction*.

Addiction, as a predator, also spawns other predators, almost like smaller animals feeding on a carcass that a bigger animal has killed. These other predators are people who profit from addiction, sell addiction, promote addiction, and supply addiction. By the time this publication reaches you, it is pretty safe to say that Black Tar Heroin is in your city, in your neighborhoods, and in your schools. "Heroin? Here? Never!" you might say. Even if you are in a rural farm town in Indiana or Kansas, your community is under attack, and YES there is Heroin in the high schools and middle schools. The word "heroin" elicits all kinds of images that are no longer true. Heroin is a party drug in America and the kids are "snorting" or smoking it. The images of a "junkie" using a syringe are no longer applicable. Heroin is now a part of youth and is prevalent in middle and upper middle-class communities.

Remember, for underage kids, it is easier and less expensive to get hard drugs than a six pack of craft beer. Alarmingly, with the increase in Methamphetamine and Heroin volume in the USA, a "hit" is about the same cost as a six pack. For those of us whose first contact with substances was a couple of beers, we all remember how much fun it was if we didn't get sick. Today, a youthful first experience with substances might be "sniffing" heroin. Let me assure you the euphoria generated by sniffing a tiny quantity of a drug such as heroin or Black tar heroin is a whole different first experience. The image of someone injecting drugs does not happen as much as we imagine. Sniffing or smoking the drug works almost as well; the addict that is injecting is in advanced stages of addiction.

Don't think that kids using drugs are necessarily deviant or troubled. Current surveys conducted by the University of Michigan indicate that about 20 percent of high school students smoke marijuana almost daily, and 75 percent use some drug recreationally on the weekends. Yes, this probably means your high school as well. Drugs are not restricted to the poor neighborhoods; conversely, the sellers know the money is in the middle and upper middle-class areas. These sellers *want* your children to be addicts, and their efforts are working.

The popular image of the Cartels from Central and South America is one of a bunch of madmen cutting heads off with chainsaws, and carrying machine guns. Make no mistake, the Cartels are among the most sophisticated production, distribution and marketing companies in the world. Remember that they manufacture, transport, import, and sell a substance that is illegal on both sides of the border. They enter a community with a low-priced addictive product, gain customers, build a wide distribution and a user base, then raise the price. Their target market is the youth between the ages of 12 and 20. They have been very successful in building a big business here in the USA.

All of my adult life, I have heard Presidents announce that the biggest problem in America is drug use and addiction. It started with Nixon and his war on drugs and has continued under each president to date. So far, the FBI, the DEA, local police, and billions of dollars in expense have had virtually NO success in curtailing illegal drug importing, distribution, and sales. Punishments such as stiff jail sentences for dealers only snag the low-level operative and have had little effect on the problem.

We, as a nation, are under attack, and we are losing. We are ALL victims of this powerful predator, and there is no relief in sight. Our government has failed to provide any solution or relief, but we can prepare our household.

We are always curious about why about one in ten kids become addicted. No one knows the answer, but most parents ask, "What have we done wrong?" Parents, you have done nothing wrong. Half of all families experience a divorce, yet half of our kids are not addicts. Many households are agitated and arguing and possibly uncomfortable to live in the same house, but not all of these kids in turbulent homes become addicts. There are just some kids who are prone to addiction. These kids, when they experience that first high, enter a euphoric state that they crave to repeat. First they start using on the weekends, and the cycle soon morphs into a daily habit. These are not bad kids, just susceptible kids. After a while the daily habit becomes a daily addiction, when the user has no choice any more. They must have the drug daily.

I think this addiction pattern has surprised the cartels in -so -far -as the volume they have created for themselves in all communities. The demand is so great in the USA, and growing, that they can't keep up. Recently, other synthetic drugs, like fentanyl, have been added to the substance to increase the power. Fentanyl is a manufactured chemical compound that does not require poppy flowers to make. Fentanyl is very powerful, and also very lethal. Even a tiny amount added to heroin multiplies the power many times. Fentanyl is a killer and is a primary cause of overdose deaths.

The Discovery

This is a big moment in every substance user/abuser's life. It is the moment when someone makes a clear and firm discovery of the user's habits. It is the moment when the secret is revealed; it is the moment when people are disappointed, and it is a difficult time for all. If you are starting to question someone's habits in your home, then it might be time to do a hard target search for evidence of drug or alcohol use or abuse.

What to look for:

1. Search the car trunk, the garage, or the basement for hidden bottles or beer cans.
2. Search the suspect's living quarters; yes it's okay to invade privacy, this is serious business. Look for one or more of the following:
    a. Plastic bags with pills, marijuana or a black tarry substance. Also it could be a white powder.
    b. Small pieces of aluminum foil with burnt markings, or a short straw. These are called trays, and it is method of inhaling heroin or other drugs from the foil.
    c. Syringes under the bed or between the mattresses.
    d. Check your medicine cabinet and see if any pills are missing. Almost any pill is used today by teens, so don't count any out. Pay particular attention to any missing tranquilizers, or pain pills, because they are the most popular.

The Confrontation

This is the hard part. If the abuser has been using for an extended period of time, they may be totally addicted. Oddly enough, the greater level of addition, the greater level of denial. The voices of addiction will be loud and clear. The user will hear those voices saying:

> "Hey, you can control this, it is not a problem."
> "You are not hurting anyone, leave me alone."
> "You do not need help. No treatment center."
> "You can quit whenever you want to."

At the same time, you are asking them how much are you taking/drinking? How long have you been doing it? Where do you get this stuff? Who are you taking it with? Let's get you some help!

Please don't forget that *all addicts are liars*! Their total focus is on getting drugs or booze and getting high. During this discovery, be aware that the information coming from the user could be totally false.

Prior to the discovery moment, make plans to get some kind of help. Alcoholic withdrawal can be fatal and should be provided under hospital/medical supervision. Most drug withdrawals are very unpleasant, but not fatal; however a number of drugs during detox are very helpful (Suboxone).

As a suggestion, following the discovery and confrontation, insist that the user stay with you for an entire day under observation. This means 24-hour eye contact with the user. The user is very crafty, so even a bathroom trip requires a search of the room prior. Don't let them out of your sight! If addicted, they will truly have a very difficult time being clean for 24 hours, and this process may tell you how serious their problem is.

If the user remains in total denial, the most definitive method to determine the extent of the problem is a Urinalysis (UA). These little test kits are available at most pharmacies, so if the user states that "I don't use alcohol or drugs!" have them urinate in the small cup. These tests can determine drug use. A person who is NOT using should have no problem complying to this simple test. The user will be very, very defiant.

I would recommend that prior to the confrontation, one develops a recommended plan of action. The usual path is to send the addict to a treatment center for detoxification, which can last a couple of weeks. Centers provide isolation from substances and some tips, tools and techniques for staying sober.

You will hear the term "tough love" again and again. This is a term that means your love is not the love of enabling, but the love of recovery. So everyone is clear, here are what might be called "tough love" actions:

- Never give the addict money.
- You have a right to ask for a urine analysis anytime day or night.
- If the addict does not comply to your wishes, you should expel them from your home and support.
- All family members should agree and follow the above three steps.

If you are the mother of an addict, you will be very tempted to "help" them in a traditional motherly way. Providing love, house, laundry, food, and money are the typical loving functions. Remember that in "tough love" the sooner the addict reaches a point of hopelessness, the sooner they will be blessed with a *will* to change. A *will* to change is the first and opening step to a pathway of recovery.

In many cases, the user realizes that the concept of being homeless and living on the streets is always a possibility. Certainly, as one travels in any major city, the homeless in America are quite visible. The addict fears being homeless. They will develop a million stories as to why you should help him/her with a place to stay. The sooner they reach the threat of being homeless, the quicker they may seek help and reformation.

If you can, try to use the "discovery" as a positive moment for the family. As a group, being positive, you can all state that you will try to help the addict deal with their addiction. Make the event a positive group effort filled with love and hope, even though you will probably be very, very mad.

The Voices of Addiction

You may think you are more powerful than booze or drugs, but you are not. Compared to addictions and the overbearing power of addiction, you are without influence. Addiction is all powerful and actually gains in strength with the passage of time. You are wasting your time if you think you can control it.

When the problem of substance abuse comes to visit in our lives, we mistakenly think that we can use logic to make it go away, that the addict will listen logically and conclude that he/she is doing harm to self. We tell our teenage child that drugs and alcohol are bad and will cause them a life of misery. We tell a loved one that they will not be allowed in the house if they continue to use. We threaten divorce or disinheritance. We cry, we yell, we beg. And yet, the person continues. And it usually gets worse. Much worse.

Although this may seem silly, logic doesn't work. The voice of addiction is just too powerful, too stimulating, too aggressive. The voice is in control, and it won't let go, it won't be quiet. It will not surrender. Most addicted people have heard a pile of logical reasons why they should not drink or use. Parents, loved ones, school, police, judges, jail, counseling, and friends try to make sense and give "warning notices." None of it works. None of it.

As you are trying to convince the user of the dangers of continued use, here is what the voice of addiction is telling the victim. The *voice of addiction* . . . Imagine those who care for the addict talking to him/her. Below is a documentation of what *we* are saying and what *addiction* is telling them. We say one thing, they hear another, just as loudly.

We say, "Don't you realize that using this stuff is hurting your body? We are going to have to get involved here and send you to some kind of treatment!"

Addiction says, "Listen and be polite, promise anything, but don't stop using me. The things this person is telling you don't really mean anything because they do not understand you as I do."

We say, "Let's get you some help! Let's ask the priest about treatment centers and how long you need to stay in there to get cured!"

Addiction says, "You have total control over using. You can quit any time you wish. I will quietly go away whenever you decide."

We say, "We have found a treatment center in California; it is expensive, but we do have some money saved for a rainy day, and I suppose this is our rainy day. You are flying out, going to stay thirty days and get the best care in the world. We love you and we want the old person back in our lives. We will beat this thing!"

Addiction says, "Okay, let's go to treatment, after which you can start using again. Hey, it's only thirty days. I have heard you can get drugs and booze in treatment anyway. Try to act like you are grateful, then do whatever you want anyway. You know best for what you need!"

We say, "When you come home after treatment, everything will be the same. We will be here to help you, love you, support you and cherish you. We are excited about the "old you" coming back."

Addiction says, "No one understands what I am doing. They do not realize that everyone is doing it; I can control my problem, it is no big deal. Everyone is overreacting! When we get done with this stupid treatment center stuff, we can come home, get a job, get an apartment, and do whatever I want. No more hassles!"

We say, "Thankfully, we think we have found a place to 'cure' you. They have to best staff, doctors, everything. It will be good, and it will be helpful."

Addiction says, "Doctors and counselors have no idea what you feel and are going through; if they had the same stuff going on in their lives, they would start using too! No one understands you but me, and I take all the pain away. Talk just won't do it."

In Treatment, we say, "We are so thankful that we had the money to send you to this intensive 28 day program. Please try to listen to the counselors and the doctors, as they will help you. They are the best in the country. Please follow all the rules, they are designed to help you recover."

In Treatment, Addiction says, "You hate this treatment center. Coming here was a mistake! The staff is terrible and always enforcing rules! I know best what is good for you. Let's make some plans to go home early. As far as these stupid therapists are concerned, I am the only thing that makes you feel really great all day. They are just full of crap! Run! Tell your parents that you are just miserable here and need to leave. Cry if you have to. To kill the time in there, you should 'Hook up' with one of the young girls. They are fun!"

We say, "You only have a week left, then you will be home and new person! We are excited about your return and have your room all ready!"

Addiction says, "Hey, move out right away! Go to another city where things will be better! Plus you won't have to deal with all the legal mumbo jumbo! Move in with the girl you met in treatment. She really seems cool, although she was a heroin addict. She at least understands me. Living with her in a new city will be like a dream, and we can use if we want to. You can totally control it! You always know what's best for you. Plus, you will have *total freedom*! Play your parents along, then 'poof' away you go!"

We say, "During and after treatment you will be familiarized with, and understand that twelve step meetings are mandatory part of your long term recovery. If you don't like a meeting, go to another until find one where you feel more at home. There are hundreds and thousands of meetings in your city. Meetings will help you recover and will be particularly helpful after treatment. We recommend ninety meetings in ninety days to aid in sobriety short and long term.

Addiction says, "Oh brother, meetings? It's impossible to sit around a table with a bunch of losers and hear their stories of their stupid lives. No way! You have much better things to do than meetings. 90 in 90? Ridiculous. Stay home and watch television, play video games and do whatever you want. Every meeting you go to, you will hate!"

Talk to the addict all you wish, but remember that as you are talking, the Voice of Addiction is screaming at the patient a constant roar of self-destructive behaviors. Some of this "point, counterpoint" is listed in the examples above, but many more exist. All the logic in the world will not influence the person. The only way for the voices to quiet down is when the user finally decides that he has had enough forever and is ready to truly engage in getting help. Until that time, words are useless. Remember that you do not have the power to influence the addict to stop. Loved ones, friends, police, court, romances, church, have little or no influence until the addict takes the first step and truly recognizes in his/her soul that a problem exists that is lethal and has the *will to change.*

As you read the "voices" above, think about how each of these statements applies to your addict. As you review these, I hope that you will come to a quick conclusion about how much influence you have over the addicted. These voices, however crazy, supply the addict with a "way out," with an alternative to what is good and healthy for them.

The true challenging and overwhelming fact is that these voices *never* leave the addict and will keep working on his sobriety for the balance of his/her life. Always there, they will quiet with each day of sobriety, and continue long-term aftercare. Each day of recovery strengthens the individual's resolve and determination. One day at a time.

What do we do? I would love to say "nothing!" but readers probably want more. If there is any part for you to play, it might be to recognize when *addiction* is talking. Addicts are just about all the same in behavior, and certainly so if they are proponents and components of the *Substance Nation*.

Most people look at *addiction*, particularly people in the treatment world, as a disease. They call it the *addiction disease model*. This is kind of a fancy term that makes treatment look very super scientific. One of the mysteries of this identification is the dealing with the *why*. If someone contracts Spinal Meningitis, few people when hearing of this disease affliction would ever ask the question *why*? Yet parents and addicts themselves are obsessed with the "*why*."

The simple answer is, on the question of Addiction, no one knows "why" exactly. What I do know, however, in a rather unpopular opinion, is that *all addicts act the same*! I think it's just as important to watch out for *addictive behavior*, more so than the actual discovery of the *substance*. Addictive behavior is all pretty much determined by how powerful the *voice* is. The main variable is the choice of substance. For instance, if someone is using opiates, including Black Tar Heroin, every day. Yes, they are an addict, and, even *worse*, they are physiologically dependent upon daily use. This level of addict, the opiate user, requires detox, and a very unpleasant first few days. Rarely, however, is detox from heroin fatal. Alcohol detox, by contrast, *can be fatal*, and requires medical detox in a hospital setting.

Okay, *what do we do*, is covered in a separate chapter with detailed action/response modes recommended. Behavior for the addict, however is pretty similar and may aid the family in recognizing the problem. Remember that no matter what the circumstances, Addict behavior is pretty consistent and mostly unmovable. Here are some firm *addict behavior axioms*.[NL 1–8]

THE VOICES OF ADDICTION

1. All Addicts are liars.
2. Stealing is okay to get money for drugs.
3. Substance is my full and total focus for the day.
4. Obtaining substance trumps the Ten Commandments.
5. Promiscuity is okay if it produces money.
6. Addicts struggle with loving themselves or others.
7. When using (other than amphetamines), Addicts seem tired.
8. Addicts are bored and defiant.

So that you know, all of these axioms are at play every day. While you may only see one or two that seem to fit the patient, these axioms are always there, and will all appear with time. Keep your eyes open.

Enabling

An Act of Love

This chapter might be for women and mothers in particular. The love you add to the world is one of the most precious gifts. Thank you. It is a pure and wonderful love, and it is never ending. What we are going to talk about here, though, is not very pleasant, and might be a powerful dose of reality.

When Addiction rolls into the home, the women hate it. It destroys the balance of the home and family. Fear and secrets abound, as all cherish the family and its integrity. The enemy is here, right here, in *my* home. Living with an alcoholic/addict is always a nightmare. It is always a test of courage, it is always a fearful journey, and it seems to have no end.

At some point, there is usually a "discovery" when the user is disclosed or admitted. This can start with a DUI arrest, or finding some drugs or drug paraphernalia in someone's room. At first there is shock, then denial, then confrontation, then acceptance, then fear. Something new and just not too pleasant has arrived. Family pride can quickly turn to family shame, or can result in the "cover up" when you hope that the neighbors or friends have no knowledge of what is going on in *your* home.

In most cases, you have wondered why the offender has been acting a little odd. Studies and athletics are abandoned in high school, new friends start showing up, the old fiends don't. Husbands miss work and other events. They have the "flu" or a "headache." A promising child that previously was headed for greatness now seems to be totally stalled and indifferent. Yes, there have been signs. We saw them, but we just didn't want to admit that something was wrong. We didn't want to challenge anyone, maybe because we just thought it would go away, or maybe we thought it was merely a passing phase, or we just simply were in denial.

None of the background is important anymore. After the "discovery" of the secret, the fear begins, the terror arrives, and our first thought is "How can I fix this problem in my home?"

More often than not, the first tendency is to become an *enabler*. No, this is not some kind of bird. Enabling is a very destructive and progressive event that many parents and especially mothers, participate in. Enabling is a participation sport with few players. Simply, someone is enabling the alcoholic/addict to continue his/her habits, but with the intent of helping the user.

Please understand, we are all guilty of enabling in this situation. Enabling is part of the disease of addiction. It is another way that intentions are twisted and turned from a goal of helping, to a result of destroying. Addiction causes the user to become a very adept manipulator, thief, con-artist, and liar. The disease needs *money* to continue, and the disease will cause the afflicted to do just about anything to anyone to finance itself. It is very, very cunning and powerful. In all cases, Addiction is more powerful than you. You do not have a chance. It is in control.

Here are some of the things an enabler will do to "help" the user.

1. Calling the employer to make an excuse.
2. Giving the user money, providing food and shelter, and other forms of support.
3. Threatening the user with the intent of overpowering the disease. Threats usually not enforced.
4. Loaning the addict money on a promise of return.
5. Ignoring or covering up theft of money or other objects to pawn for money.
6. Sending adolescents to treatment centers when they have no intention of being sober.
7. Defending the addict's actions in accidents, arrests, and overdoses.

Each one of these topics could generate a full chapter on their own, but I think you see what I mean. Our intention is to be helpful, but our actions extend the addict's ability to obtain the substance of choice. I am sure that you have heard the statement *tough love*.

Tough love is cutting the addict off, forcing them to stand on their own, bringing them to a faster bottom, and in effect, "helping" them to obtain sobriety. Refuse money, refuse to call the employer, refuse to lie for the afflicted, don't send them to treatment, send them to the street. This is tough love and it is the most positive thing to do.

Remember that if you have a child that is using drugs, every dollar you give them, every meal you provide, the shelter, the help, may lead to an overdose, and death. If you love them, let them go. Let them find reality. For a mother, this is the hardest thing to do for your child that you nurtured from birth till today. The disease of Addiction is more powerful than you and you cannot defeat it by fueling it. You defeat it by starving it.

And *oh boy*, you are going to hear a lot of great stories. If someone in the family has an alcohol/drug problem, you will not believe the stories you will hear so that the person will be able to continue with their habits. Here are some good ones:

"AA? I can't go to AA! What if someone from work will find out? I will lose my job!"

This is a good one, the only problem is the addicted is not considering the real problem, which is what happens to their job if they keep drinking or using? Hello?

"I don't have an alcohol/drug problem, I just can't sleep and I have to have something to help me relax. If I could only relax on my own!"

Common excuse, however, it does not take like *ten* drinks to relax.

"Mom (Dad), I need to borrow some money for school (car tires, clothes, etc.). I really need it."

Hint: the money is not for school or anything productive. It's for drugs.

The addict will appeal to extended family members or friends as well. An uncle, aunt or even a neighbor will be targeted for a "loan." Remember here, this is not the real person that is trying to gain finance, it is the addiction. Addiction has real power.

The number-one sign that your child has a problem is the continuing issue of *money*. Addicts need drugs daily, and they cost *money*. You may begin to wonder, "where is my jewelry?" or "why is my bank account balance lower than I thought?" I know that you are thinking that your child would never be pawning your jewelry or stealing from anyone, and normally that may be true, but the lure of drugs is so powerful that people will easily turn to theft to buy them and use them. This is true regardless of your financial condition. Many middle—and upper-class patients of mine confess pawning something of value, such as an heirloom wedding ring. Against addiction, values melt.

ENABLING

The addict develops a tendency to project all blame onto others. They will find themselves in trouble. Legal, financial, personal, and emotional problems. They will tell you all about these problems, almost as if you caused the problem, or as if you can solve the problem, but never with the realization that the addict themselves *caused the problem*. Somehow they seem to feel that we are going to alleviate the situation, whatever it is. Almost every time, our role, as they see it, will be to provide money to help make the alleged crisis situation dissolve. Every time, however, this money will be used for drugs, and more drugs. Every Time.

There is a mantra from Al-anon regarding addiction—"You didn't cause it, you can't control it, and you can't cure it." Keep this in mind and let it guide your actions.

I have added this story to this book at the last moment. This is an anoynomous story of a daughter who was an addict, was treated with "tough love," and now has recovered and is best friends with her mom now. This is her story unchanged and unedited:

> Well with all the post today so many suffer. So I thought I would share my story. I went through so much I would quit and start again. My mother showed me tough love; I didn't get to go back home I had to live my life in the way I chose to. Don't think she never worried about me because she did. But she chose to live her life not mine. At 28 years old I tried to shoot so much dope to end my life, but that didn't happen, god had other plans, I had been raped I had beaten people and been beaten myself. I was a ticking time bomb. At 30 I had nothing not my kids not my house no friends nothing but a suitcase, I was at my dealers house I had just gotten high and in that moment I got up hit my knees and asked god for help. The next few days happened so fast my grandmother had me a spot in rehab I was in my way, I was there a week and I got arrested, for the first time in years my mom answered her phone to me from jail she said don't lose hope, I went to court the next day and the judge let me return to rehab. I had a great counselor I was ready. 4 years ago I lost my son at 28 years old he committed suicide from a drug overdose, he had gotten paralyzed at 18 in a car wreck and he never recovered from it. I lost my boy to drugs. Oh the guilt I felt, and my daughter she is 25 hooked on that life style. I spoke to them many times about drugs and the loss, they didn't listen. The other 3 kids are not using and doing ok. I raise my granddaughter and I have been given a gift, I did end up with HEP C and I took the new medication and have been cleared for years. I am now a nurse and I have compassion god gave me my

life back and he will do the same for yours if that's what he wants to do. So please live your life don't live your child's and give them to god. My mom did and I've had to and yes I lost one I know he doesn't suffer anymore. Yes I miss him everyday I have memories and I have the love of my little boy. That's what he will always be my little boy. But today I live my life you never get another chance. My love and prayers to all of you."—Anonymous

This letter was taken from an addiction website, and I included it here as an actual example of how people's actions have little effect on the addict. In this case, the mother decided to live her life and not her daughter's.

SECTION 2

When Addiction Strikes

The Lethality of Money

So that we all understand, realize that an addict, particularly a hard drug addict, cannot just "decide to quit" without consequences. Withdrawal and Detox is very unpleasant, while most users will self-claim that they can "control" their habit and "quit any time I want" few things could be further from the truth. Generally, the addict has no real intention of ceasing drug use, and they will do *anything* to continue being high. *Anything* is a very big word, and it encompasses a large selection of actions and reactions.

Simply, addicts have to have *money*. Finance is the cornerstone of continuing with their addiction, and while using, no rules exist, or any code of honor that would interfere with finding *money*. Your loved one, that you may have raised since birth, will be transformed into an extremely cunning, focused, and evil thief. Somehow, drugs change the logic process, and the importance of getting "high" outweighs adherence to any ethical or legal codes. Patients in my treatment sessions reveal some of the terrible things they did to friends and family to obtain money and are mystified how their behavior was so altered. Stealing money, Grandmother's wedding ring, laptops, lamps, jewelry, televisions, anything that can be taken to the pawn shop.

The pressure to obtain money to buy drugs is not once in a while, it is everyday all day. Gaining money can also include prostitution with both sexes, armed robbery, bad checks, everything you can imagine, and even more than you cannot imagine. In some cases, when the addict has a partner, one of them will enter prostitution so they both can continue buying drugs.

Parents love their kids, and just about everybody wants to help someone in trouble. Mothers, aunts and uncles, a friend, a cousin, a neighbor may believe they are helping the addict by giving him/her money. The addict may have a magnificent story of why they need some finance. Broken down car, sick girlfriend, surgical expenses, paycheck coming, boyfriends father died and we need to go to the funeral, deposit for an apartment, or just a "loan". Every dollar you give to an addict will always be used to obtain substances. Money is Lethal!

Today, drugs are cheap! Black Tar Heroin costs about ten dollars for a small amount. This is about the same as a six pack of specialty beers, and, if you are under twenty-one, heroin is easier to get than alcohol. Most of America is in denial, but heroin is everywhere in our land. So, if you give an addict just twenty dollars, you have given them enough for several injections. You may have even given them the ability to buy the drug that they overdose on and die. Never give an addict any money.

Drugs tend to fluctuate in popularity from decade to decade. The last big drug craze was *methamphetamine*, and it's not over yet . Easy to smuggle into the US from Mexico, easy to manufacture or "cook" if one has some technical skills and some materials. Meth has a very powerful and effective distribution network, and some areas are still in a pitched battle with this drug and its consequences. Someone can become both psychologically and physiologically addicted to this drug in a few weeks. *Meth* is not an opiate, and does not sedate, but has the opposite effect. The user feels blissfully energized and optimistic for as much as eight hours, until the effect is slowly metabolized by the body and the euphoric feeling wears off. As will most all mind-altering drugs, however, there is a "reverse effect" when the drug wears off. The user then is filled with sadness, depression and a general sense of foreboding that is very unpleasant. The greater the addicts use level, the greater the "coming down." The user then is compelled to use Meth again to chase the previous feelings and return to a "high". Some states were overwhelmed by the volume of this drug coming into their communities, and Meth has been the number one drug problem in America.

While the high from Meth is wonderful, the drug, with long-term use, causes mental and physical problems that can result in lethality and insanity with long term use. I would say that, in simple terms, this drug "scrambles the brain" and long-term addicts tend to lack solid judgement or sound thinking processes. Most meth addicts will chart general nutritional, mental, and physical deterioration.

Beginning with about 2013, Black Tar heroin arrived on the scene, all coming from a province in Mexico. Black Tar, or "black" is processed opium, and it is very inexpensive. Couriers from Mexico can carry tens of thousands of dollars of product in a small valise or under their clothing. Sometimes this drug is "cut" with other more powerful synthetics such as Carfentanil or Fentanyl, which makes the dose stronger and sometimes lethal. Most dealers that have distributed marijuana or cocaine now sell this killer drug as well. Small size, low price, and super addictive makes this the perfect drug to sell.

At some point in an addict's life, they will more than likely turn to "dealing" drugs in order to afford their continuing habit. Black tar is a natural item to market, and it is highly profitable. Dealers can easily make enough money to support their habits, but requires a slightly different lifestyle than just being a plain addict. Along with dealing can come violence, robbery, visibility, and imprisonment for long terms. For the parent of a dealer, the signs are pretty simple and recognizable. Here are some:

1. Strange people may be coming to your house, replacing the old friends that visited.
2. Lots of phone traffic.
3. Mysterious behavior and times of disappearance.
4. The sibling may stop asking for money and will still be buying things.

Money is the pathway to drug addiction. Money is poison. Stopping the money flow will help to stop the addiction, particularly if you are providing the finance. Please never think that by giving a loved one money that you are helping them. You might be killing them. The probability of overdose is increasing, due to the addition of fentanyl, to both heroin and meth. Fentanyl is a synthetically produced substance produced right across the border in Mexico. This drug adds a great deal of power to other drugs and is extremely concentrated and dangerous. One common event in today's drug world is a person who has been in detox and treatment will relapse with an injected dose at the same volume as previously used. Their bodies have adjusted with the time of non-drug use, and the dose may be more powerful than expected. This is a cause of overdose deaths, and overdose is becoming quite common in the drug world.

The Electric Avenue

As if the current problem of drug availability, and use and abuse of hard drugs isn't enough, enter now the world of personal electronics. The iPhone from Apple did not hit the market until the summer of 2007, so the concept of carrying around the internet in your hand is sort of new. Billions of these phone/internet devices are in people's hands worldwide. No one has to really search for connectivity, it is all coming to you every day, all the time. Music, Games, Texts, Movies, Tweets, Blogs, Personal recordings, Pornography, Audio Books, everything comes along with the phone. It is a common site to see the young, and the old, totally engaged in texting or viewing something on their handheld instruments in public. Once a person hears that little "beep" of a delivered text, the phone might as well be on fire in their pockets. The desire to look at ones phone seems to be overwhelming. In the evening and at other times during the day, many people spend hours in front of their computers.

Scholars studying society and psychology and human development contribute contrasting statements about how all of this electronic based activity might affect our society. I suppose we need a little more time living submerged in a computer driven world to decide the true impact on mankind. One aspect that I think everyone agrees upon, is the fact that this "electronic focused" part of modern living is *addictive*!

Psychiatrists, Social Scientists, and Psychologists all struggle with how to define, understand and treat this form of addiction. Electronic addictions are new and have truly emerged in the last few years. One thing that I am certain about, however, is the fact that this type of addiction is based upon the desire for *entertainment*.

A little more than a hundred years ago in America, our entertainment was maybe a newspaper in front of a fireplace. People used to spread information also by talking and sharing news, ideas, stories, etc. About the

1920s or so, the radio became the most common electronic in the home. Everyone would crowd around the radio for news and entertainment. I think the radio kind of replaced the fireplace. The radio might have been the first invasion of entertainment by electronic devices. The radio, of course, was followed by the television as a focal point for the family, and later cable television, offering expanded content. The television was pretty much nationwide by the end of the 1950's. Sometime around 1980, the personal computer arrived. The next forty years or so have been advancements in capabilities, reduction in size, and expanded software offerings. Today, even a small hand-held phone has the ability to view the world thru the internet, and is a fully capable communication and information tool. I see people sitting stone cold quiet in restaurants, never talking, but eating, with one eye on their cell phone. People under thirty, live as if their whole world is in their phone.

Recently, while consulting on the campus of a major university, I was traveling a few floors up in an elevator with seven students. Usually, people always look up at the numbered floor indicator, but not here. All the students were in that Neo-Classic posture, looking downward into the cell phone, with fingers at the ready. I could not help myself, and I said "Hey! All of you people look like intelligent, bright, and fun students! I think you should all talk and get to know each other instead of staring into your phones! What do you think?" The students were, I think, startled about the "old man" talking on the elevator, then they looked up at me and laughed. The next second, they were staring at their phones again. Go figure.

The reason that I am writing about the Electronic Avenue that entertains so many people is not necessarily addictive, but also to demonstrate how Americans are so inclined towards *entertainment*.

Americans are just nuts about being entertained. It seems that we crave it so much that our entire lives are always seeking it. We have drawn our lives around the concept of being sort of swept away from the mundane and simple. Even a meal that we all enjoy at home around a table has been replaced by a "jump in the car" and going to a fast food establishment. Sorry to tell you this, but most of these fast food places serve products that kind of taste like cardboard. "You deserve a break today" actually means "get in your car, burn gasoline, and get a meal high in salt, fat, and additives." Entertainment.

Okay, we have seen how being entertained is a big part of our lives. Now, consider this: *alcohol, cocaine, pot, meth, hallucinogens, and opioids are also entertainment*. Boredom is just not something that we can handle easily, so a quick way to entertain ourselves is by using a substance. I believe that boredom is the direct opposite of entertainment and is a key reason many people use substances. Almost all of my patients say that the key reason for their relapse is boredom. We might want to start looking at life, and days in the life, as being a conflict between a desire to be entertained, versus being alone and quiet. With all the surroundings in modern America, some people cannot stand being alone for even a few minutes.

When someone goes to a treatment center or enters intensive outpatient treatment for substances, they are looking for a cure. They want help and they want to change their lives. The problem here is that treatment never deals with how to overcome boredom, and how to lower the desire for entertainment. What they find is 12 step meetings, protocols to change your destructive thinking, yoga, relaxation therapy, exercise, etc. *None* of these protocols address boredom and a desire for entertainment. You will notice that a patient who is addicted to alcohol or/and drugs will always have this strange attitude/exterior screaming "entertain me!" In many cases, the patients approach to treatment is one of expecting something to happen to "save them." The attitude of assuming that something, someone, or some exercise will magically recover them to a sober life is a problem. The patient that enters treatment with the idea that they have to engage in the process, has a strong will to change, and surrender their ego will have the best results. One has to WORK to recover.

Many hard drug patients, especially those that have been in multiple treatment centers, seem to have the attitude of "hey, I do not want to be here anyway, so I will just sit here and let you try to help me." I can tell you this patient type is the hardest to work with. Frankly in these cases, nothing I say or do will be more powerful than the lure of a drug like heroin. I just cannot overpower the constant thought in the patients mind of the euphoria these opioids provide. By the way, if you are thinking that you can talk to a loved one and somehow "shout" louder than the lure of drugs, you are wasting your time.

Treatment protocols will have to be refocused and reinvented. Learning how to relax does little to help to a patient that has a very high expectation of entertainment and is bored with the treatment process. Patients need to process and understand their needs for entertainment and learn to be at peace with themselves. Today, there are no effective treatment protocols to alleviate boredom.

The Evolution of the American Family

IN THE NOT-TOO-DISTANT PAST, America was an agrarian nation. Prior to World War Two, most people lived in rural areas, on farms. Everyone worked. The family was a unit, a team, and an organization. They ate, slept, played, worked, worshiped, talked and lived like a team. The family was a farming labor force without which the farm would not produce anything.

We had a dairy farm. I can still remember my mother coming into the kitchen in the morning with her apron full of eggs she had just secured from the hen house. My mom could cook anything, and she made gravy for *everything*. I think she used a pressure cooker daily, as I remember the spitting sound of it in the afternoon. The pressure cooker seems to have disappeared, and so have certain dinner items such as dandelion greens, brains, tongue and corned beef. The pressure cooker tenderized all of these "less than prime" items.

Later in life, we lived in a middle-class subdivision in a small town in Indiana. Everyone I knew was pretty much the same at home. Dad worked, but Mom stayed home, Dad drove an older car, and Mom had a new one, the homes were three-bedroom ranches, a grandparent or two lived with us, and the kids were going to be the first to go to college. When we got off the school bus, one or more of the neighborhood moms would have cookies and milk waiting for us. Not boxed cookies, fresh baked. Chocolate chips were the favorite. We never came home to an empty house. We would play by the river in the woods until dark, then return home for a family meal together. No one had any debt beyond a mortgage. No credit cards, no second mortgages.

Today, some fifty years later, things have changed. Both parents work to survive, neither one has a new car, the grandparents are in nursing homes, and none of the kids are planning on going to college unless you have a scholarship or financial aid. When the kids come home on the school bus, they arrive to an empty home, and when the parents come home from work, they are too tired to cook or talk, so a pizza is delivered and all watch television or play video games. There are few conversations, as we are electrically entertained.

As the Substance Nation (refer to previous chapter) grows in numbers, kids are going to be tempted to "experiment" with alcohol, pot, meth, cocaine and heroin, along with the pills secured in the bathroom medicine cabinet (behind the mirror). KIds are coming home unsupervised, energized, and out of control. Parents don't arrive home for hours. The youth is totally vulnerable, in danger, and looking for a thrill. Enter the dragon. There is an old tale claiming: "Idle hands are the Devils Workshop"

So we have seen a disintegration of the family structure, communication, and maybe respect and honor along with it. The seeds of Addiction are planted, and they are growing. Most of you are thinking that your child is not susceptible or corruptible. We all want to think we are different and that our family would never make self-destructive choices, we think our loved ones would never do anything as stupid at use drugs. YES, every parent has thought this, but in reality probably one out of every five kids under 18 are using drugs or drinking alcohol to excess. One in five.

Some might ask, "How can we tell if our children are using?" Here are the *most common signs of drug use and abuse*:

1. Fatigue: the drug user will seem to have lost all energy and drive. They will stay in their room in bed more than normal.
2. Sports disinterest: drinkers/druggers lose interest in sports quickly. Practice is just too much of a bother, and training gets in the way of using.
3. Friend change: the old friends will slowly disappear, and new ones will appear. Youth who do not use will not want to "hang out" with a user. They will quickly drift away.
4. Mysteries: money may disappear from purses, hiding spots etc. Addicts need money, every day. Jewelry may come up missing. If several incidents of missing valuables occur, you have a problem.
5. Falsehoods: remember *all addicts are liars*, and their falsehoods are a "cover up" for the truth of Addiction. Somehow, Addicts become the

masters of stories and explanations. Most stories are possible but not probable.

6. Romantic relationships disintegrate: this will happen quickly, since a girlfriend or boyfriend will know about the secret drug or alcohol use and will not want to be around it for long.

If you suspect that your loved one is using regularly, then the first step is probably *the search*. Some might say, "Searching someone's room is a violation!!" Yes, that may be, but I say this: "*If my intent is not to shame or punish, but to help, then I sure as heck can search whatever I want to in my home.*"

If a search is warranted, and suspicions are high, then I will search high and low for any telltale signs of drugs or alcohol. Most addicts will hide their supply somewhere, as the supply is coveted and necessary. Under beds, car trunks, closets, drawers—nothing is off limits. Find it and confront the user. You might be saving their life, not violating their space.

Also, asking a child in your home for a Urinalysis (UA) is *not* a violation of trust or respect. I feel you have a *right* to demand one. Hey, if the person is not using, they should have no objections. You can purchase urine test kits at the drugstore and they are accurate. This demand may meet great resistance but may save someone's life.

Family Dynamics

This topic should probably have its own chapter, as it is worth paying attention to for your family relationships. When Addiction comes to visit your family, the dynamics and relationships change quickly. What was a normal peaceful environmental relationship can be filled with uncertainty, anxiety and a redefinition of roles. Lets use a family of four as an example. Here is what I mean by dynamics changing.

- Normal: the family composed of father, mother, son 16 and daughter 15. The daughter is "discovered" as having a drug/alcohol problem.
- The father: he will feel that he can "control" the situation and "cure" the problem with warnings, orders, and anger. He is extremely frustrated at his ineffectiveness and helplessness. His focus is now on the daughter, and the son receives much less attention.

- The mother: motherly love becomes focused on the user, often Mother will become the "soft parent" and possibly begin to enable the daughter with support, money, etc.
- The son: he is left out of the issue and relatively ignored compared to the past. He may begin seeking more attention by excelling at school or sports, or doing just the opposite, He is anxious, uncertain, and lost.
- The daughter: she is the addict, so she is very, very, manipulative. The addict will "play" this new family scenario by appealing to her mother for funding and sympathy, telling the father any lie necessary to maintain her freedom to use, and enjoying the extra "love" and attention she gains from the addiction. Somehow, addicts have an innate ability to take advantage of the new family dynamic.

So the roles of everyone change quickly. The general result is that the group is now outside of their normal and regular roles. The family feels uncertain, anxious, angry, disturbed and resentful of this new structure.

If you are experiencing this type of dynamic transition, you will note that the result is anger, shouting, frustration, and a general sense of hopelessness. Unfortunately, this is normal. The family must learn to recognize, discuss, process and accept these new temporary roles, establish boundaries, and unify. This might require separate counseling for the family in general.

The family, in summary, becomes very confused and frustrated. The father becomes angry with the addict and himself. He has no control over the abuser, and often has angry outbursts. The mother, in an attempt to show love and compassion usually helps enable the addicted with money, food, lodging, and sometimes harmful attempts to make the addict "happy." She has pain in the relationships with her family members and usually feels that she has "failed" as a parent. The newly arrived addict becomes very adept at manipulating everyone to aid herself in obtaining drugs or alcohol. The child that is not using feels ignored and abandoned. Often this child may start excelling at school or activity to gain more praise and attention, or begins to do the opposite. Both positive and negative reactions usually will secure more attention from the parents or close family members

The picture of today's family seems to be dramatically different than even just a few years ago. It seems like the family structure and the solid foundation of the family is under attack from several quarters.

First, with both parents working, the children are less the focus of the adults. The parents may be becoming "self-centered" rather than "family-unit centered" and living more stressful lives of trying to earn income as well as raise a family.

Second, the world of electronics and the Internet, cannibalize the time the family used to spend in a connected manner. Connection and communications are now minimal.

Third, many families are experiencing the use of substances. Parents drink more, take tranquilizers, anti-depressants, smoke pot, etc. The children are not experimenting with drugs about age 13 or 14, and maintain their use secretly. So family members now have *secrets*.

Fourth, families living in the suburbs used to be "safe" from drug dealers and "pushers." In the last five years or so, the marketing of drugs has swung from the inner cities to the suburban and rural areas. These new areas are under attack.

The factors that affect the family create a great deal of uncertainty and anxiety for all in the family. Change is not always an easy thing to tolerate.

The Genetics of Addiction

Psychiatrists, Psychologists, Geneticists, and people in the addiction treatment profession all debate whether or not there is such a thing as a "genetic disposition" towards addiction. Everyone wants to try to understand why some people are more prone to addiction than others, or somehow "inherited" their problem,

Statistics suggest that about ten to fifteen percent of all individuals chart addictive behavior. In the USA, with some 330 million people, 30 to 45 million individuals possess an inclination towards addiction or are currently addicted to a substance.

If you are concerned with the "why" of addiction, and have a desire to determine causation, the first place to start is with the families of both parents.

Did anyone in the family tree suffer from alcoholism or substance addiction? Brothers? Sisters? Uncles? Aunts? If so, it might be that the entire family may tend to become addicted. The caveat here is that even though one may have addicted relatives, there is no absolute tendency to become addicted. So, yes, it seems that this behavior might be handed down the family tree, but not always.

Most people who are struggling with addiction usually site an uncle, grandfather, or some relative that was an alcoholic. Some might think that "okay, that is the reason you have a problem." If we look at the odds, however just about everyone will have an alcoholic in their family tree. Consider the family of grandfather, grandmother, dad, mom, uncles, aunts, sisters, brothers, cousins, etc. Most people would have ten or more relatives in the tree, so statistically one in ten will be a substance abuser. Prior to about twenty years ago, alcohol was the main drug of choice, so more than likely, everyone would have a family member addicted to or abusing alcohol. Of the one in ten in our nation that have a substance use disorder, only one of those will seek treatment.

Trying to spend time trying to understand why someone has a problem seems fruitless. Learning why does little good. Spending more than a few seconds trying to determine "how" or "why" a person has a problem seems like a waste of time as opposed to spending time on what we are going to do about it!

Why is so-and-so this way yields us very little helpful information. Every addict and alcoholic has one thing in common, they began with tiny quantities, and the amount grew and grew. The second thing they all have in common was that the substance really made them feel good. Every person abusing a substance started with a quantity that made them feel wonderful. The problem is that larger quantities are required to "chase" the original feeling.

As part of a diagnostic, that is to say, evaluating whether or not a person has a problem with substances, it is probably a good start to look for some telltale signs. Specifically, these are behavioral changes; as the substance becomes more of an obsession with the individual, their behaviors change dramatically. They may start:

- Missing days of work
- Showing secretive or mysterious behavior; having grades slipping in school
- Isolating from family and friends Finding new friends with bad habits Hiding substances and alcohol "Zoned out" on the weekends
- Weight gain or loss
- Becoming non-communicative: Disappearing for parts of the day or weekend Anxious or Depressed appearance
- Daily or regular use of substances

If you are seeing several of the behaviors above, it is likely that the person is moving towards or experiencing full addiction. At this point "why" is not really important. An addictive person uses drugs and/or alcohol to self-medicate anxiety, depression, or some mental illness. Usage starts at low levels and develops into a full force addiction. The only "why" we really need to understand is the fact that all substances require larger and larger quantities physiologically to deliver the desired results. The addict starts with one dose, drink, pill, snort etc. Euphoria results, soon the required dose doubles, then triples, and so forth.

Requiring larger doses is an absolute and alters behavior. The afflicted begin to spend time in an obsession to obtain more and more of the substance. Time, relationships and finance are often affected, as the focus in life is on drug seeking and obtaining. If you suspect someone of being addicted, take them camping for the weekend and never leave their side, you will see withdrawal working in great strength. Addiction is constant, pervasive, and it never sleeps.

Once family members realize that addiction has come to call, the question is always "why me" or "what have we failed to do" The solid answer is *nothing*. Someone with a substance problem is no one's fault, no one forced this person to use, your actions are innocent and nothing you have done has caused someone to self-medicate. That is the good news! The bad news is that there is little you can do to make them stop! Positive actions are discussed in book two of this trilogy, *Treatment Talk*.

If you have an adolescent with a problem, remember that it is not your fault. Adolescents always experiment with substances for a thrill. Today, it is a normal part of growing up in America. Some continue using for years, then stop, but some of them become addicted. Adolescents who are addicts have allowed the "experiment" to become an everyday event. Adolescents are prone to self-medication as these years of maturation are a mental challenge to all. Self-esteem, the power of peers, acceptance, and physical changes stimulate a certain angst in all teenagers, and substances are an instant method to "take away the pain."

From ages 13 to 19 or so, emotions are on the surface and self-confidence is in question. In previous decades, the standard first experiment was a couple of beers or shots, followed by giggling euphoria, followed by vomiting.

The issue today is the prevalence of drugs such as prescription painkillers, marijuana, ecstasy, cocaine, and heroin. The first experiment may be sniffing black tar heroin, instead of three beers in the woods, so the first experience is at the top of the euphoric index. Drugs that can become physiologically and mentally addicted in a few weeks may be the first experience. Shockingly, the volume of some drugs, such as heroin, brought into the USA brings the price of a dose to less than a six-pack of craft beer.

In schools, these drugs are generally quite small physically, so a middle school kid can easily bring "hits" of drugs to class. These substances can be used without anyone knowing, unless the student begins to demonstrate unusual behaviors. Yes, your schools have drugs, all of them.

So this chapter started with the question of whether or not someone can be genetically disposed to drug or alcohol addiction. The answer is *nobody knows*, and we should probably not get tangled up with trying to figure out why someone has a problem. If you prefer, then *yes*, the problem is the same as Bob's Uncle John, he was an alcoholic, so it runs in the family. Statistically, about ten percent of all Americans are addicted to something, so the odds are in favor of someone in your heritage being addicted.

Section 3

Conclusions and Considerations

The Twelve Steps of AA

Fighting Addiction

IF YOU ARE ENTERING the world of addiction with a loved one, the one thing you will hear, over and over again, is the term "the Twelve Steps." In fact, if you are a patient in treatment, you may just be absolutely sick of hearing these same three words. When a young patient enters treatment, virtually every center will start patients in the Twelve Steps of Alcoholics Anonymous. The hope here is that the patient will engage in this treatment modality, which requires the patient to complete each step, one at a time, and work towards the goal and inference of each individual step. Wait! These twelve steps were not developed in some University Psychological think tank, they come from Alcoholics Anonymous from 1935. This society has no profit motive, is not involved with any cause or issue, and is solely dedicated to aid people in *not using*. Any of the groups in AA, or any other self-help group, is totally dedicated to living drug-free. These groups are a united bulwark against the Opioid Crisis, and addiction in general.

Along with working the steps one by one, the patient is usually required to find a local sponsor, and also start reading the "Big Book" of AA. The essence of AA, and its singleness of purpose is often missed in the process. Through the twelve-step process, the participant is hoped to realize that *they* are the problem, and that *their ego* is the destructive force in their lives. Addicts fail to live for the day, they live in the future, self-generating anxiety and fear, or they live in the past, self-generating guilt, shame and regret. Peace is found by surrendering to someone else's will other than your own, and by learning to live in the present. The member experiences a process towards losing their own will, and allowing life to "just happen" I realize that this process sounds a little dreamy, but there seems to be a distinct moment when the promises of AA are delivered. This moment is when the person begins the road to recovery.

Those that are resistant never seem to engage in the program or reach any kind of long term sobriety. One of the ongoing problems with younger addicts is that they have had the Twelve Step program presented to them so many times that they reach the conclusion that "Twelve Steps just won't work for me!" I suppose that I can testify that for sure, the program worked for me, although it took me many years of just going to meetings before the concept of dropping my ego and will finally sunk in.

Let's look at the most critical of all the steps, Step 1. It reads: "We admitted we were powerless over alcohol or drugs, and that our lives had become unmanageable."

This little step seems pretty innocuous, One might think, "sure I really need my booze and my drugs, and my life is not turning out very well." On the surface, this would seem like an easy step to read, digest and move to step two; *absolutely it is not*! If someone is able to digest the fact that they are powerless, and truly accept it, only an insane person would ever use substances again? Right? When someone relapses, it is pretty safe to say that they had not accepted the very first step of the program. The first step is the foundation for all the other steps, and one has to truly realize that they are powerless with an unmanageable life.

When one admits in their soul that they are powerless, then they realize that substances have taken over control of their lives that addition has created the unmanageable portion of their living. This is form of basic surrender from a person that has thought that they were in charge of their lives and always knew "what was best for them" In reality, the substance was controlling what the addict did each day, that he was powerless, and self-destructive.

It is not mandatory that the individual totally "surrender" when they first encounter this step, but it is important that one begins to give their will up a little. If the patient can just realize, a little bit, that their will and thinking has created all of their problems, the healing process can begin.

So we are all clear, the Twelve Step program is not just reading the steps or a book. This program of recovery requires several firm and absolute adherences to the following:

- Get a Sponsor
- Go to Meetings

THE TWELVE STEPS OF AA

- Read the Big Book of Alcoholics Anonymous
- Don't Use Substances

When someone says, "The Twelve Steps didn't work for me" the odds are very high that the individual did not follow the path very well. The Twelve steps did not fail, the *person* failed to follow the path of recovery. Always remember, the addict will find a thousand reasons *not* to attend a recovery group of any kind. Some of the excuses you will hear are:

- I feel out of place there.
- I can't stand hearing people talk of their addiction.
- I just don't fit in!
- I don't like to talk in front of a group.
- I just do not get anything out of it.
- I am just too tired at night.
- It's too far to drive.
- The meetings are so boring.
- The room is too hot.
- The room is too cold.
- I can't smoke during the meetings.

I think you get the idea here. One can invent many reasons *not* to attend meetings! My message to these people that struggle is simple: *find another group*. I mentioned that here in Phoenix, there are 1600 meetings a week all over the valley. 1600! I think one can find at least *one* that they like. Keep searching!

Go online under recovery and a list of all the meetings in your area will pop up. Unless you live in a very rural environment, there will be a meeting near where you live. Sometimes these meetings will be the gateway to sobriety, without attending any type of treatment center. Many have entered recovery through these meeting rooms. To those we say—congratulations, while you are not alone, you have successfully engaged in this treatment process and willingly wanted to change your lives. You have made it work!

Frankly, I have had a fairly long experience with these meetings, and to this day, all I can say is "for me, it is working!" I have no idea how or why, but they do work. And, of course, they are free. Please note that there are several kinds of "anonymous" meetings, all pretty much utilizing the same principles. To name a few, there is Narcotics Anonymous (NA), Heroin Anonymous (HA), Gamblers Anonymous (NA), Overeaters Anonymous (OA), and many more.

Every meeting I have attended starts with some readings, one of which is usually The Promises of AA. These promises are the pledge of AA that if you follow the AA or NA path, certain things will be delivered to you. Here are the Promises:

- Promise 1: We are going to know a new freedom and a new happiness.
- Promise 2: We will not regret the past nor wish to shut the door on it.
- Promise 3: We will comprehend the word serenity.
- Promise 4: We will know peace.
- Promise 5: No matter how far down the scale we have gone, we will see how our experience can benefit others.
- Promise 6: The feeling of uselessness and self-pity will disappear.
- Promise 7: We will lose interest in selfish things and gain interest in our fellows.
- Promise 8: Self-seeking will slip away.
- Promise 9: Our whole attitude and outlook upon life will change.
- Promise 10: Fear of people and economic insecurity will leave us.
- Promise 11: We will intuitively know how to handle situations which used to baffle us.
- Promise 12: We will suddenly realize that God is doing for us what we could not do for ourselves.

These Promises are powerful claims, providing a new way of living in the world. More importantly, as we read these rather haughty promises, we should realize that *these promises are delivered to those who follow the AA (NA) Program*! If these promises were *not* delivered, the meeting rooms would be empty, and the fellowship would disappear. These promises are absolutely delivered to those who follow the program or there would be no AA at all.

Also please note for those that claim that "AA just doesn't work for me!" and never had these promises delivered in their lives, I would suggest that they just *did not work the program* with any commitment or honesty. It was not the AA program that failed, it was the patient that failed.

A strong message to all addicts, alcoholic or drug, is that *no one* can attain sobriety and serenity alone. If you are in treatment, when you graduate, you will need to go to support groups *for the rest of your life*. If you are serious about recovery, then you will need support. There are "all women" meetings, "all men" meetings and meetings of all kinds. Sorry, there are no drinking meetings. As one looks to the future in recovery, they will be told to live "one day at a time" and that is good. Just remember that you have to include a support group meeting in that day.

The Damage of Secrets

At the end of this Trilogy, I cannot help but include some statements about what the best things for a family might be to *prevent* addiction. Most addiction counselors spend a lot of time searching for some type of trauma, or mental affect that might be at the core of substance abuse. Once they feel they have determined the event or period of time in one's life, then they focus on the feelings surrounding it. Next they attempt to captain the patient to process the event and move past it. All of this psycho action may or may not prove helpful, and, of course, every person is different and requires individual treatment. Sometimes the patient has been addicted for so long that much of their life is in a blur. Some of the young patients I have treated, under twenty-five years of age, have been using heroin daily for *ten years*. They have truly missed much of growing up and adolescence. They entered what I refer to as the Substance Nation and have lived apart from mainstream America. Some professionals observe an event in a young person's life, such as a wild divorce, and peg that as the "cause" of someone's addiction.

If divorce were the cause of addiction, *half* of America's youth would be addicted, and that is *not* the case. Some look to a parent's substance use or abuse as being some kind of genetic predisposition that leads the youth to addiction. The problem with this is the fact that probably half of America drinks alcohol and/or smokes pot, yet half of the younger set are not addicts. I would contend that there seems to be some issues within today's family that might spawn addiction, or at least boost the possibility of it. This is my opinion, but here it is anyway. Specifically:

Secrets: A family cannot be healthy and balanced if they have a lot of secrets. Secrets block communication, trust, and family health. Infidelity, money problems, problems at work or school, disappointments, grieving, relationships, health problems, or substance use and abuse are often never discussed in the family. The person maintaining the secret is living with a falsehood, or indiscretion, and the rest of the family has suspicions and anger. Often issues such as the death of a loved one, addiction, relationships, etc. are never discussed or processed within the family group. The concept of keeping secrets fuels the person that has developed a substance addiction to hide it and keep it secret.

Often, there is a lot of effort in keeping a secret. Depending on the type of issue hiding can almost be a full-time obsession. If the lines of communication are open within the family, then anyone can reveal a secret and the rest of the family will assume a helping role. The longer the secret is maintained, then the discovery of it will fuel anger and disappointment for all. The statement of "why didn't you tell us this a long time ago?" sums up the family's frustration.

Monkey see, Monkey do: Adults in the family often smoke and drink and maybe smoke pot daily. The casual use of substances is a regular event in the household. The kids are told, "don't drink or smoke or take drugs," yet the parents do it in plain sight and daily. The message here is clear. "Substances are okay if you are an adult!" Right, except your kids are getting the general message that drugs and alcohol are harmless, and when they go to a party and are offered a sniff of heroin, they try it. Sampling is the beginning of addiction. Grownups, please try to make your consumptions less obvious, unless you are ready to accept your kids following you. You may not have a problem with alcohol or drugs and you can stop anytime, you have drinks after work to "relax." Fine, that may be true for you, but it may not be true for your children. When they experience their first drug or drink they might be "off to the races." You will suffer the consequences, so if you can quit, why not quit today?

The Rebel Child: Hey, we were all probably a little bit rebellious during our teenage years. Rebellion is just a part of growing up. During my adolescence, I supposed a rebel would have a hairdo, a hot rod, and smoke cigarettes. We look at this sort of "Fonzie" type individual as being part of American culture. Today, we have the same rebel, but the definition has changed. I noticed in the mid-sixties and beyond, the high school quarterback lost his position as being the social center, and the drug dealer took over. The boy who had all the substances and was a rebel, became the hero. This is still in place in many high schools. Today, this same person has access to meth, cocaine and heroin and in reality, is a *danger* to the culture.

Drug acceptance groups exist in high schools and colleges, and this is the source of the Substance Nation denizens. These drug groups fear nothing when it comes to using drugs, mixing drugs, and even overdoses. There will *not* be an end to these drug users until the kids decide to end it in conjunction with the parents. They will have to formally identify drug dealers in the schools and develop an honesty and open communication with their families. At the same time, adults in the family are going to have to stand up for their communities and get involved.

So the "rebel" has been redefined and refueled with harmful substances. I think the adolescent has a normal tendency to be rebellious, but today this rebellion can take on a very perilous road with the addition of powerful drugs.

These three instances are conditions that I think help develop addiction. Most addicts begin using in their teenage years. There is evidence to suggest that using alcohol or drugs during the years before turning twenty-two or so actually alters the brain chemistry as it is still developing. The individual seems to throw some kind of genetic switch and alter the brain so it will crave substances for the rest of one's life. Whether or not this chemical alteration is true or not makes little difference. We all know that young people using alcohol or drugs leads to death, addiction, prison, treatment, accidents, overdoses, and chaos. That's enough for me.

AMERICAN OVERDOSE TRILOGY
Conclusion

I TRULY HOPE YOU have seen some benefit from these three books on Addiction. I have tried to deal with three major topics as briefly as I could. *American Overdose* deals with the national problem of drug availability and what affect it is having on our culture. *Treatment Talk* is for those who are considering going to or sending someone to treatment, the different types and alternatives, and what to know before you go. *Killing Family* is a reprint of portions of the original text addressing the impact addiction has on the American Family.

    I suppose the main motive for the creation of this trilogy is the fact that most people are totally helpless when addiction comes to visit. I have tried to equip the victims of addiction, not just the addict, but the family and friends of the addict with some type of plan of what to do. Alongside the advice of what to do are written suggestions for what *not* to do. I pray that my words will somehow make this tragedy easier to survive.

Kent I. Phillips

www.ingramcontent.com/pod-product-compliance
Lightning Source LLC
Chambersburg PA
CBHW062027220426
43662CB00010B/1510